No Mom Jeans

A deliciously witty guide for new moms who want to ditch the sloppy sweatpants and embrace mommyhood with style

Melissa Fiendell

Published by Next Chapter Productions, Cincinnati, OH

Cover and interior designed by Jamie Runyan

ISBN: 978-0-9848689-1-9

Printed in the United States of America

First Printing, 2012

FOR ALL THE amazing mommies --- and all that you do for your families, your world, and yourselves.

Contents

Introduction

AFTER ATTEMPTING FOR nine months to stylishly disguise my ballooning waistline, kankles, and increasingly blotchy complexion, the big day finally arrived. The years of waiting, months of daydreaming, and hours of screaming had finally come to a magical, perfect end. I had become a mother. As I looked at my sweet little angel, I knew life would never be the same again.

After getting over the astonishment of literally being handed another life to take care of, my husband and I brought our little bundle of joy home. We laid her in her pristine designer bassinet and spent what felt like hours fawning and cooing over her. All bundled up in her carefully selected home-from-the-hospital outfit, she looked too adorable for words. We were absolutely dazzled. Fast-forward an hour or so. We were still sitting there gazing at her. We start exchanging nervous glances as if to say, "Umm, now what?" After a few more quiet, almost awkward, moments my husband looks up at me and offers, "… how about a trip to Target?"

So off we went with our three-day-old daughter. We picked up diapers and, when my husband inevitably wondered off into the electronics department, a couple cute new outfits to clad all seven adorable pounds of our sweet baby girl.

Before we left for the store, I remember gazing down at the mess that was me and contemplating what a girl three days post-partum is supposed to wear on her debut trip out of the house as a new mommy. I was (thankfully) no longer in need of the 12 inch stretch tummy panel in my maternity jeans, yet (much less thankfully) not even close to hoisting my pre-pregnancy Sevens over my new child-bearing hips. Beyond clothes, my hair hadn't been colored in nine months, or even washed in four days. My skin was broken out and definitely lacked that pregnancy glow I had been waiting forty weeks to receive.

I threw on a fuchsia velour tracksuit, swept my greasy hair into a sloppy ponytail, and prayed not to run into anyone I knew. My husband drove, if you consider gingerly easing the car forward at about 10 miles an hour driving. I sat in the back seat, lovingly watching over our new addition and fiercely trying not to glance at my new big girl thighs. They stared back at me begging to know why I had crammed them so tightly into such a hideous, brightly hued fabric that really would have been better suited for pajamas.

Who was this person? Not only did I feel totally unprepared for motherhood, I suddenly also had growing fears of mom jeans, dark eye circles, and a permanent muffin top. Would I soon trade my coveted handbag collection for a big sloppy diaper bag and a practical, over-the-shoulder faux leather purse?

As it turned out, what to wear was only a fraction of my worries. At home, my swanky contemporary décor was about to become overwhelmed by primary-colored, plastic chaos. In the morning, my beauty routine was about to be shortened considerably, when not discontinued altogether. Even my deepest relationships were about to take a turn for the very different. Fashion aside, was I starting to lose a part of 'me'?

As I searched for ideas and solutions to become the modern new mom I aspired to be, I was disappointed to find very little help. After being inundated for the past year with advice on how to have a fabulous, stylish pregnancy I expected to find similar information for my new life as a mom. But gone were the dedicated magazines, clothing lines, and websites. Once I had turned the bump into a baby it seemed that I was on my own. This was new territory, and I felt totally unprepared. I was overwhelmed and full of questions. How will I find time to cover my dark eye circles and do my hair? Does the giant baby swing have to sit in the middle of my living room? Is motherhood a good excuse to stop shaving my legs regularly? Will I ever be able to leave the house again? How long will it take me to lose this baby weight? Is it possible to be a new mom and still be stylish? Does any of this even matter anymore? Do *I* even matter anymore?

Apparently once the baby comes you are on your own style-wise and, if you're not careful, about to enter a world of 24/7 tennis shoes and one too many conversations about the consistency of your baby's poop. But it doesn't have to be this way! With desire and a little bit of effort, you can have the stylish, fabulous life that every new mommy deserves. You can keep some of your pre-baby moxy in your post-baby world. Doing so will help you feel more refreshed, confident, and energized to bond with your baby and care for your family.

I'm not a nutritionist, former fashion model, or celebrity. I don't hold a PhD in child development or pretend to be a baby whisperer of any sort. The suggestions in this book are not based on years of schooling or professional training. They are simply a result of my experiences. I do have a background in the beauty industry, a 24/7 addiction to HGTV, and a healthy obsession with fashion and everything style-related. I've also been blessed to connect with thousands of mothers across the world, and hear their thoughts on many of the topics in this book, through my work with Pampers. Most importantly, I am a new mom and I am a woman. I love my little girl, but I also have interests, passions, and ambitions that reach beyond changing diapers, warming bottles, and playing peak-a-boo. The contents of this book were inspired by what I have learned trying to balance living in the world of *mom* and the world of *me*.

With the birth of my daughter, I discovered a love and passion so intense that sometimes I feel like it has literally engulfed my entire self. It fills every crease and crevasse of my body, my heart, and my soul. Sometimes I find myself wondering if I am capable of loving anything more than I love her. Yet in the midst of all this joy lives uncertainty, confusion, and sometimes a nagging sense of loss. When we become mothers are we simultaneously losing our old selves? I felt as if I was saying goodbye to the woman I'd spent the last twenty-nine years trying to get to know. A big part of me resisted this. To become a good mom, did I have to give up being the woman I am?

After my daughter was born, not only was I feeling confused and alone, everyone I knew suddenly wanted to share their favorite new mother horror story with me. It seemed each woman was trying to out-do the last and scare me into believing my life was over. One after the other told me that once you become a mom you won't have time to shower, will lose your desire for sex, dread traveling, and morph into Porky the Pig. Instead of sharing tips on how to cope with new parenthood, most women I spoke with focused on telling me how tired I was going to be and how impossible it would be to leave the house, let alone blow-dry my hair.

They were right. And they were wrong. I was tired and it was hard to leave the house. I did feel fat and trying to wash my hair at the beginning was tricky. However, with a bit of creativity and a lot of positivity, I found ways to embrace and actually enjoy new motherhood. By the time my daughter was six months old she had been on ten airplanes and camped in a tent. She was the youngest guest to ever stay at a quaint B&B in northern Minnesota and had ruined her share of hotel crib sheets. She accompanied me to dinners, picnics, and even the occasional trip to the nail salon. She learned to entertain estheticians while I got a quick brow shaping. She watched her dad and I play tennis at the park. Together we experienced music classes, baby gyms, and swimming lessons. I even got to watch my sweetie experience her first celebrity crush when Kendra and Hank Baskett randomly showed up at our gym class with their adorable little heartbreaker, Hank Jr. We learned to eat, sleep, and play comfortably in less than 1000 square feet of living space. Some days we dressed up and went to parties, and others we stayed in snuggled up in our jammies. Within three months I was in better shape than before I was pregnant and rarely let a day go by without getting dressed and putting on a little makeup.

I share these experiences not because I want to brag or fool you into thinking new motherhood is glamorous or easy, but because I want you to know these things are all very possible. My daughter was far from a perfect baby. She had more than a few public meltdowns and was barely sleeping through the night at six months old. Nonetheless, together we were adventurous and tested out new activities and routines. We learned what worked for us (a game of peek-a-boo while I deep conditioned and exfoliated) and what didn't (baby yoga classes).

I have learned that not every new mommy story needs to be negative and not every mommy needs to be a martyr to her family. You can still take care of yourself, maintain a strong relationship with your spouse, and live in a home that does not resemble a circus tent. You have the power to choose what you want in your life both before AND after you have a baby. You do not need to give up all aspects of yourself when you become a mother. If you love to travel, you still can. If you enjoy dressing up and doing your hair, keep doing so. Doing what you love may take a little longer and require a bit more planning now that you have a little one, but it is still absolutely possible.

I learned quickly that maintaining pieces of my old self was as critical to becoming a good mommy as perfecting a swaddle, checking the bath temperature, or getting my little one to latch correctly for a feeding. By prioritizing myself and my needs, along with those of my baby, I discovered the balance I had been searching for. I realized within one woman there is space for many roles. You can be a mother, wife, employee, and friend. You can still indulge your passions and make room for the rock star, author, fashionista, or homemaker you want to be. Having a child means that being a mother is now a huge part of your life, but not that it is your entire life. And it certainly does not mean that you need to stop brushing your hair and start wearing homemade socks with Crocs.

Some say that it is selfish to focus on yourself and that you should be completely focused on your baby. I disagree. I believe that by taking care of yourself you will be better equipped to care for your baby. That when you look good, you feel good. That when your home is in order, your mind and life follow along. I think that by keeping your relationship with yourself healthy, you keep your relationship with others equally esteemed.

The advice in this book comes from my experiences. Take it for what it is, one woman's opinion. I certainly don't have it all figured out or do it all right 100% of the time. I have learned some lessons that have made my new mommy life easier, and even a little bit more fabulous. I hope the words in this book help you to look and feel your very best. I hope you embrace this next chapter of your life with an adventurous spirit, an open heart and mind, and a fierce new mommy style that is all your own.

CHAPTER 1

Fashion

YOU'RE A MOM. Since when does that mean you have to give up being fashionable? Having a baby doesn't require dressing like June Cleaver, or worse Kate Gosselin (back during her still with Jon days). However, your new lifestyle will require a bit of a wardrobe shuffle.

During maternity leave, your previous Monday-to-Friday work attire will be retired and replaced with a more practical but no less stylish closet of chic, urban mom essentials. With a few new pieces, you will look great even when you're just lounging around the house. If you re-enter the working world you can do so in style with flattering outfits that scream polished and professional.

The beginning of motherhood is a great time to pitch old, ill-fitting garments and invest in a short list of quality pieces that you will cherish almost as dearly as your adorable little munchkin over the years to come. This is also a good time to toss anything that trends a bit more tacky than chic. This includes your collection of slinky 'for when I go to Vegas' numbers (you know the ones I'm talking about) and old undergarments.

Replace old gear with a few classic sexy pieces for date nights with your husband and ladies' nights out. Top off your look with some fun accessories, and you will be ready to tackle mommyhood in style.

Lounging

Spending more time at home does not mean you need to transform into Frumpelstiltskin and start parading around in your husband's t-shirts and old boxer shorts. Nor is this license to spend the day in the nightgown you slept in, wearing your two-prescriptions-ago glasses. Do yourself a favor and cleanse your closet, pitching or donating anything that you could have worn to high school gym class. Warning: If you leave these things in the house they will unassumingly climb on your body and linger there until you start to like the way they feel. Get rid of them! Seriously. Do it now. Instead, spend your lounging days with your new mommy booty clad in relaxed sophisticated style.

I discovered my inner hoarder after my post-baby closet cleanse. I found it hard to actually part with many pieces, no matter how gross or old. But after donating eight (okay, ten) large garbage bags full of icky, stained items, I felt lighter than ever. Not only could I actually see all the great items that remained in my closet, I had removed the temptation to ever again wear my Grad '99 hoodie in the 21st century.

Yoga pants - The best thing to ever happen to modern female lounge wear is the yoga pant. You need to own at least one pair even if you have never muttered the word "Namaste" or ever care to experience the circulatory benefits of downward facing dog. The best part of the yoga pant is the softly appointed, somewhat generous waistband that hugs your middle as if to say "what muffin top?" Your pants should be snug everywhere except the waistband and an inch or so too long in the leg. With all the wear and washing these pants will get they will climb up to the exact right length in no time. If you can keep yourself to buying just one pair, opt for basic black. Black is slimming, a great disguiser of baby spit up, and looks polished with a monochromatic top or a bright pop of color. When it comes to yoga pants, you cannot beat *Lululemon* for quality, style, and comfort. No matter what size or shape your booty, a pair of *Lulu's* will give you the best looking behind you've had since grade school. Think Kim Kardashian meets Kelly Ripa fabulous. If you happen to be the one woman who does not fall in love with these pants, check out *Alo* or *Hard Tail* for some alternative styles.

On-trend sweatshirt - No over-sized kangaroo hoodies here! You are looking for something comfortable and cozy with heavy dose of modern chic. The best options are not big and baggy, but instead somewhat tailored to your body. Narrow sweatshirts in your size are actually much more flattering and better at hiding a few extra rolls than their baggy counterparts. An extra-long slim fit with a cut out boat neck is a great option to lengthen a short torso or camouflage a not quite back in shape booty. Just make sure the cut is slim and waist skimming. For the more daring, a tight sporty version with a front zipper and pouch pockets made of thick Lycra or cotton is another surprisingly slimming option. *Nike, Adidas,* and *Lululemon* all make great zip-ups in a variety of fashion forward colors and styles. Try to avoid anything extra baggy. If you can imagine your father wearing it is not allowed on your hot new mommy body!

Everyday

Look effortlessly chic everyday by mastering the art of layering. Aside from looking great, layers will keep you cool in a world of post-partum hot flashes, help to camouflage a not yet toned tummy, and make nursing on the fly a cinch. Stock up on these three new mommy layering essentials.

High quality Lycra-cotton tanks - Invest in more than one. These will become a dressing staple especially if you are nursing and even more so if you are brave enough to do it in public. Classic black, grey, cream, and white are always in style and go with just about anything. Look for versions with a built-in bra to give your twins some extra support. *A Pea in the Pod* sells phenomenal tanks specifically designed for nursing mommies that have built in tummy control and a clip strap for easy access to the girls. Even if you are not nursing, the extra support in these tops can be great for eliminating post-pregnancy belly jiggle and keeping your ladies standing at attention. In terms of durability and quality, you get what you pay for. You will be wearing these tanks a lot, so opt for higher quality if you can. However, if you are breastfeeding and a leaker (you know who you are), you might consider lower-cost brands, since your tanks might end up being more disposable than you anticipated. You might even consider purchasing an extra tank or two for bedtime. I learned this lesson the hard way after my husband woke up in the middle of the night trying to figure out which one of us peed the bed.

Long, loose cardigan sweaters - Unless you are braver than most, parading around in a spaghetti strap tank top weeks after delivery is probably not something you are excited about trying. Enter the wrap cardigan. This sweater adds a cozy layer of warmth with impeccable style. It can be worn loose, tied, or wrapped around your midsection to deemphasize your post-natal belly. An extra billowy sweater with lots of fabric can also double as a nursing shield for on-the-go breastfeeding. *Splendid* and *Free People* make lovely wrap cardys in a variety sumptuous fabrics and colors. *Merona* has similar and equally fabulous sweaters at super affordable prices.

With two sets of grandparents in living in a different country, airplane travel was a big part of our life post-baby. Oversized, soft cardys quickly became my best travel companion. They added an extra layer of warmth on drafty planes, doubled as a baby blanket, and acted as a wearable nursing shield for discrete feedings on long flights.

Scarves - A well-placed scarf has been a style statement across the globe for decades. It remains more fashionable than ever today. The beauty of a scarf is that it adds dimension to your outfit and can be appropriate in any season. Light as a feather, tissue-weight cotton creates a breezy, romantic vibe for summer. A traditional pashmina with a seasonally appropriate splash of color is an effortless spring and fall classic. Thick woven woollies create cozy style all winter long. In a pinch, a scarf can also be useful as a mop for baby drool or the occasional bit of spit up. Do yourself a favor and buy versions that are machine washable.

On the bottom it takes just a couple of closet basics to create your everyday look. You won't regret investing in these simple stylish pieces.

Black leggings - Before you rip out this page, I am not talking about that pair of your mom's 80's stirrups. Always say no to shiny spandex, especially when foot straps are involved. The leggings of today are a great casual alternative to jeans and are easily dressed up when paired with a breezy shift dress and a pair of boots. When it comes to selecting your sleek leggings, the thicker the better. Ideally you want them to have a bit of structure to contain your butt and thighs and a little stretch to hug your curves. The right pair of black leggings is infinitely slimming, lengthening, and go with just about everything. Check out the legging collections from *Juicy Couture* and *Banana Republic.* For a less expensive option, peruse your local department store's tights section. Many brands like *L'eggs* and *Hue* have created lines intended to be worn solo as leggings.

Your favorite pre-pregnancy jeans - Just because you had a baby doesn't mean you have to part with your favorite pair of baby blues. Keeping your old jeans in the new mom fashion rotation is not only a great incentive to get your body back into fighting shape quickly, it's also a nice way to keep a little of the 'old you' in your new mommy world. If you can't quite button your favorite pair yet, do not despair. There is help awaiting you in a little magic piece of stretchy heaven called the *Belly Band.* A *Belly Band* is the ONLY part of your old maternity wardrobe allowed back into your new fashion rotation. This ingenious little fabric band silently conceals a belly bulge and makes your temporarily tight jeans feel just like your favorite old pair of sweats. If your favorite pair are a little on the long side to accommodate your previous life of 24/7 heels, consider having them professionally altered to a length more appropriate for flats. You will (sigh) probably get more use out of your jeans if they don't require a three inch heel. If you can't bear to see your favorite pair hacked up consider buying a second pair with a shorter inseam. This gives you a fabulous option for date nights with your sky high stilettos and an almost equally fabulous option for every day.

To finish off your contemporary casual style, the right pair of shoes is the icing on your fabulous fashion cake. Every hot new mommy needs four key pairs.

Slip on sandals - Sandals are a great go-to summer and spring closet staple. They combine practicality with easy to wear style and complement almost any bottoms. The most basic option is a simple flip flop or slide. To turn up the style quotient try a more bohemian look with a pair of bronze metallic gladiators or flat funky dark leather T-straps. If a simple thong style is more your speed, consider purchasing yours in an unexpected color or with a unique detail. A shiny clasp or a little sparkly faux crystal trim will add interest to your outfit. Above all, make sure you are choosing a pair that are reasonably comfortable and can be slipped on without much effort. Ideally you should be able to put them on with no hands, leaving both free to hold to your baby while you are trying to dash out the door.

Athletic - Rather than a traditional pair of jogging shoes opt for a more urban sporty version made popular by our friend across the ocean, the pedestrian European fashionista. Look for a shoe with a low, sleek profile that could comfortably nestle underneath a pair of jeans without looking bulky. Both *Diesel* and *Puma* have nice selections that are equally stylish and athletic. The most important thing about this pair of shoes is that they are incredibly comfortable. These will be your go-to pair for impromptu play dates and power walks with your baby. While style is important, there is nothing fabulous about sore feet. Having to endure a foot full of blisters every time you go for a walk to shave another inch off your post-baby booty will not make you a happy mommy. *Merrell, Aerosoles,* and *Rockport* have been bedrocks of the comfortable shoe category for years, and luckily, these brands no longer limit themselves to your grandmother's styles. All have a nice selection of surprisingly stylish options that will have your feet believing they are walking on little pillows of luxe cotton straight from shoe heaven.

Tall flat leather boots - Nothing says fabulous like the perfect pair of tall leather boots. These puppies add oodles of style to just about any outfit from maxi dresses to A-line skirts to leggings or jeans. Opt for a pair with either a flat sole, a slight wedge, or up to a 1 inch heel. Avoid adding extra stress on your joints and skip the high heeled boots. While you may have been willing to sacrifice comfort for style in your pre-baby life, the daily marathon that you now run will have you rethinking that balance pretty early into mommyhood. Purchase your boots in a basic neutral like black, dark brown, tan, or grey. Avoid the temptation to spring for a fabulous pair in crimson or banana yellow. Even though they are equally fabulous you may tire of a flashy color quickly. These boots will likely be on the more expensive side of your wardrobe, so it would be tragic to get sick of them given your potentially hefty investment. *Born, Miz Mooz,* and *Franco Sarto* make great sturdy boots that will last for more than a few seasons. If investment quality is more your style, splurge on timeless pair from *Cole Haan, Frye,* or *Stewart Weitzman*.

During my maternity leave I was determine to find *the* pair of flawless flat boots. Since I planned on wearing them a lot and was willing to spend a little bit extra on a long-lasting pair, I refused to settle for anything but perfect. Quickly I learned that trying on dozens of pairs of boots with a baby in tow was a bad (terrible) idea. Enter *Zappos*. I started ordering boots three at a time. I would try them on at home and return the ones that didn't work. It was smooth sailing until the first four figure credit card bill that sent my husband into a tailspin before I explained I didn't spend that much money on one pair of shoes. [I made a mental note to use my private credit card for all future *Zappos* purchases.] I'm embarrassed to say it took a half dozen tries. But with *Zappos* fast, free shipping I found the perfect pair in just over a week. The best part was that I didn't have to endure the struggle of keeping my baby busy while I tried them on, never mind the embarrassment of returning over a dozen pairs of boots to a real person. Even better, the returns were a quick drop off at the

UPS vs. trucking my baby to the mall to stand in a long department store return line.

Ballet flats - Ballet flats are a terrific option for adding quiet sophistication to a casual everyday outfit. They don't dress down your look the way athletic shoes can nor do they give the impression of trying too hard the way a heel does in the daytime. These shoes do such a nice job of working with most anything in your wardrobe you may want to pick up more than one pair. Having one pair in a solid and another in a funky pattern will bring a new dimension of fun to your closet. Ballet flats do not have to be expensive, so enjoy experimenting with an array of colors, styles, and patterns. *Nine West, Ciao Bella,* and *Kelly & Katie* all make great selections of reasonably comfortable and outrageously stylish flats that will have you skipping with glee even with a screaming baby in tow. While ballet flats are downright adorable they unfortunately are not always the most comfortable, especially if you have high arches. A quick solution is to pick up a pair of cushy insoles. For most women a pair of *Dr. Scholl's* gel pads will do the trick. If you have especially sore feet, now may be the time to consider investing is some custom orthotics.

Date Night

Being a mommy does not mean you can't dress up and turn some heads now and again. Forget now and again, do it often! Relationship experts recommend spending dedicated 1:1 time with your spouse at least once per week. If you are going to invest the time, you might as well look hot doing it. Your sexy style will help keep his mind off talking about your little darling's feeding schedule, poop, and super-adorable baby babble. Instead it will remind the two of you of the connection you share as a couple and the magic that made your little bundle of joy in the first place.

Make an extra special effort for your first date night. This will set the tone for how you will think about getting out of the house with your man in the future. I'll never forget the look of, I think *relief* is the best word for it, on my husband's face on our first post-baby date. I found my favorite pre-baby dress, with a clever empire waistband that hid my extra bit of middle and low neckline to show off my new, um, assets. I donned my tallest heels and walked down the stairs feeling like every bit the woman I was before I became a mommy. I think in his (and maybe all men's) mind there was worry that motherhood would transform his wife into the kind of woman that would rock high-waisted pants and a scrunchie. It was fun proving him wrong.

Keep the sparks alive with these head turning date night fashions.

Little black dress - Every girl, mother, and grandmother needs one. The two keys to the LBD are that you feel AMAZING when you put it on and that it is age appropriate. As a new mommy you can certainly still rock a tight little black number, but you should pay attention to the hem length. Make sure it isn't too short. Any more than 3 inches above the knee and you are getting into dangerous territory. While you will certainly get your man's attention he might not be thrilled with the mother of his baby parading around in a frock that reminds him of Britney getting out of a limo. Even though that dress probably would have worked like a charm to pick him up in your younger college days, it probably won't have the same effect today. Super short outfits are better saved for his eyes only at home or for a little post-date lingerie.

Kick-ass heels - A classic stiletto is the absolute best shoe for a night out on the town. The stiletto adds instant sex appeal to any outfit, makes your calves look toned and amazing, and creates the illusion that your legs go on for miles. When it comes to color the sky is the limit. For the more conservative mommy black, grey, metallic, nude or cream (never white) are easy options. For the more adventurous a pop of color, hint of shimmer, or a little shoe bling adds extra oomph to your look. From *Steve Madden* to *Jimmy Choo* there is no shortage of fabulous sexy heels in this world. Try an online site that has advanced search criteria like *Zappos.com* or *Endless.com* to easily filter through options and find your perfect pair.

The right attitude - No matter what you are wearing nothing is sexier to your man than his lady in high spirits and up for adventure. Even the hottest outfit doesn't mean much if your attitude stinks and you spend the whole date complaining about how sleep deprived, fat, and icky you feel. Bring an open mind and adventurous spirit to your nights out and you will leave feeling energized and reconnected to your spouse. You don't have to spend every date night all dressed up at a fancy restaurant to have a good time. Great dates can be had grabbing ice cream, seeing a Broadway play, bowling at a dive bar, going for a walk, or playing a game of tennis. If you do opt for something more casual, this is no excuse to be a fashion slouch! Wiggle into that curve-hugging tennis skirt for your match or choose a plunging V-neck when you hit the lanes. Your everyday fashion items can play double agent on casual date night. No matter what you do bring your winning attitude with a killer frock to match and watch the good times roll.

At Work

For those mommies heading back into corporate America, the only thing scarier than natural child birth is trying to fit back into your pre-baby work attire just a few months post-partum. Do not fear. With a few clever pieces your colleagues will be gossiping that you must have used a surrogate. Feel fabulous in these new mommy work must-haves.

Structured blazer - The absolute hands down number one way to camouflage a little extra weight, especially around the middle, is with a jacket. To create a beautiful, narrow silhouette and appear perfectly proportioned look for a jacket that nips in at the waist and has a little bit of darting. You can pull off a blazer no matter how formally or informally you dress for work. For more casual environments look for a jacket in a more relaxed material, like distressed corduroy or thick jersey cotton. For a more formal office, opt for a traditional blazer in a sophisticated color like charcoal, burgundy, chocolate, cream, or black.

Tailored shirt dress - No you cannot wear your husband's oversized shirt as a dress. The answer is still no even if you add a waist-cinching belt. You can however show off your fabulous self in a menswear-inspired shirt dress. The shirt dress conceals countless flaws and has the bonus of being a one piece outfit that is both effortless and comfortable. The ideal dress should fit close to your body and be made of hefty fabric. It should be thick enough to conceal bumps and bulges yet still have enough give to gently glide over your curves. If you have a naturally small waist, look for a dress that can be belted or has a belted detail built in. If you are thicker around the middle, select a dress with a V-cut neckline or leave the top buttons open – but just one or two, you are still at work!

Patterned blouse - A subtle, tasteful pattern can actually camouflage a bit of extra weight by distracting the eye with loads of pretty, playful colors and shapes. Larger women should opt for larger patterns, while petite women should look for something equally teeny. Look for a pattern that incorporates a neutral color like gray, beige or black to make it easy to match with other pieces. If you can find a blouse with a large, pronounced collar snatch it up! It will further help to elongate your torso and make you appear longer and leaner.

Straight leg trousers - Look for a pair that fit you snuggly across the hips but do not pull across the front. If the pants fit in this area and you can breathe when you button them you most likely have a winner. Next check that the leg falls straight down from the hip without any bulges or bunches. The pants should fall about three quarters of an inch above your shoe. Don't be concerned if they are too long. A seamstress can easily tailor them to your exact inseam. If you are trying to conceal those last few pounds look for pants with a wide waistband and a (slightly) higher rise to keep everything tucked in. A faint vertical pin stripe is a nice detail to add interest and create the illusion of a longer leg line. *Express, Club Monaco,* and *Ann Taylor* all have nice lines of well-fitting, work appropriate pants. If those places fail try a major department store like *Macy's*.

Pumps - Pumps are a nice choice for office footwear because they offer most of the benefits of a stiletto without as much of the pain. Look for a pair that is a balance of style and comfort. If you can muster it, try to choose a heel that is a least one and a half inches high. Any shorter and you will look stumpy and awkward. If you simply can't handle an inch and a half, invest in a fabulous pair of flats instead.

Unmentionables

Have you ever seen those super sexy magazine ads for lacy nursing bras? Please! If I had a million dollars for every new mommy I've met that got excited about dawning hot lingerie just after having a baby, I'd be really, really broke. Not to mention how many times you need to wash nursing bras to keep them clean and, um, fluid free. While I certainly wouldn't recommend going out and purchasing a drawer full of lacy thongs and uncomfortable underwire, there are a few tweaks that you should make that will add a healthy dose of style to your skinnies.

Get rid of anything gross - You feel icky enough after having a baby. Don't make it worse by dressing your body in unflattering, old, or ill-fitting underwear. Throw away anything that is more than two years old, discolored, or yucky in any way. Invest in seven sets of matching bras and panties, one for every day of the week. Seven will be more than enough. With a new baby you will be doing laundry way more than once a week. Owning seven pairs will guarantee you will always have clean, matched unmentionables.

Wear a bra - This one sounds pretty obvious but you'd be surprised how many women run out of the house with their girls just a flapping. Yes when you become a mother you do lose a bit of your modesty and, especially if you are nursing, you may spend a lot of time in and out of your bra. However, this is no reason to flaunt your merchandise for public consumption. If you must go braless try to keep it to times when you are at home alone. Bras also are hugely beneficial in preventing saggy granny boobs so use them to your advantage. Keep your ladies supported now and they will thank you later.

Invest in a bra that fits - After giving birth, a woman's body changes, including her breasts. To make sure you are wearing the best size for your new body, get a professional bra fitting. Avoid the sixteen-year-old associate at the mall and go to a reputable boutique for an appointment with a fit specialist. You will get a better result and probably feel much more comfortable in the process. If you are nursing, put off buying new bras until you are finished as your breasts will change in size and shape again. Instead invest in two or three well-fitting nursing bras. These bras make feedings, especially in public, much faster and less hassle. If you are active (and all hot stylish mommies should be!) also consider a new athletic bra. You are looking for one that keeps bouncing in check but is not so tight that it constricts. A bra that is too tight can lead to nasty new mommy conditions like plugged ducts or mastitis. Avoid these at all costs!

Boy shorts - A few pairs of boy shorts are a comfortable alternative to traditional panties and can double as cute, comfy pajama bottoms. These are also phenomenal for keeping 'everything' securely in place those first few weeks post-partum. Enough said.

Accessories

Keeping your outfits current and on-trend is easy and inexpensive with the right accessories. A few key items can also make life as a new mommy simpler by eliminating time consuming mommy maintenance. For example, a great pair of shades hides tired, make-up free eyes. Likewise, a stylish hat keeps locks that haven't been washed in a few days a secret between just you and your baby.

Stylish diaper bag - Newsflash! Diaper bags do not have to be an ugly bulky mess anymore. Today's bag designers offer a wide range of hot styles, fabrics, patterns, and colors that look surprisingly purse-like. If you really play your cards right, people may even assume you are carrying a fabulous tote instead of a diaper bag. This is your goal! Don't hide your bag in the bottom of your stroller or trunk. Use it to make a statement and swing it proudly on your shoulder like it is the amazing handbag you have been coveting for months.

When selecting your diaper bag, be careful with busy patterns. You want to find a bag that is flexible enough to coordinate with your stroller, baby carrier, and a variety of outfits. For that reason I tend to prefer solid color bags and look to the strap or hardware to add extra pop to the look. Always try the bag on to make sure it is comfortable to carry. Bags with a single thick strap or a cross body strap are usually your best options. Some even convert to a back-pack style for more burdensome trips like running through an airport. If travel is a big part of your life, look for this feature when selecting your perfect bag.

If you are anti-diaper bag, another option is to purchase a stylish everyday handbag. If you go this route, look for a roomy style like a hobo with a waterproof liner and plenty of pockets, including one that would fit a bottle. (The cell phone holder is often a perfect fit.)

Fabulous bags can be found from the thrift store to the couture shop. No matter what your budget there is a stylish diaper bag in your price range. *Skip Hop* makes a nice line of simple bags that are sure to please most mommies. For those craving more style and luxury check out *Timi and Leslie* for an unreal selection of fabulous arm candy that will make you wish you needed more than one. For the best selection, shop online for this new mommy essential.

Friends laugh when I tell them that as a 'push present' my husband bought me a diaper bag. Even more so when I tell them I actually thought that was a great gift. My cobalt bowling duffel was a gorgeous addition to my everyday look. However, as I got more comfortable I found I didn't need a giant diaper bag on most outings. Soon I was throwing a few key essentials into my pre-baby handbags. For the most part, those bags worked just as well.

Mini travel pouch - You actually do not need to carry EVERYTHING in your diaper bag all the time. This is where the mini travel pouch comes in handy. A small waterproof travel case containing a couple diapers, travel wipes, and changing pad is a must-have new mommy essential. This little travel pouch should fold up to no bigger than about 12″ x 6″ x 2″ and weigh very little. For short trips, especially when you leave knowing baby already has a full tummy, you can get away with carrying just this travel pouch plus a pacifier, burp cloth, and teeny extra baby outfit in your regular handbag. *J.J. Cole* makes well-designed travel changing pads that come in a nifty case that can easily double as your travel pouch. An oversized pencil case from a trendy stationary shop can also do the trick.

A fabulous hat (or 2!) - Hats are an effortless way to add style to an outfit while simultaneously hiding a bad hair day. The right hat can shave time off your morning routine and make any outfit look infinitely more fabulous. I like to have at least one go-to hat for each season. For summer a simple baseball cap looks crisp and fresh, provided it is relatively new and clean. For fall and spring a classic fedora in either black or khaki flatters most faces and updates any everyday outfit. Winter has so many fun lid options it is easy to find at least one that flatters your face. If you live in an extra cold climate, a fuzzy dark leather and wool number with earflaps is great option. For everywhere else, a simple cotton toque in cream, brown, or gray will work nicely. If you are one of those mommies who thinks no winter hat looks good on you, try a universally flattering knit cap with a small front brim.

Urban bandana - A nice alternative to a hat in the summer months is an urban bandana. Unlike its western counterpart, the urban bandana doesn't need to be tied. It stays in place much like a headband, secured at the back with gathered elastic covered in stylish fabric. The urban bandana is a great way to disguise unwashed hair, keep loose tresses away from baby's eager fingers, and add a dose of easy style to your everyday or lounge look. Yoga studios and lifestyle shops are great places to find your perfect bandana.

Oversized sunglasses - As a new mom there will be at least a couple sleepless nights that make even the idea of leaving the house more painful than the day your milk came in. To stylishly recover the next morning, you need a pair of great oversized shades. Blondes look great in gold or deep brown tones while brunettes look amazing in steel, grey, black, or brushed nickel. Red heads are lucky and can get away with just about anything except dark black. The only rule with sunglasses is that they are only to be worn outdoors. No wearing your glasses inside. You are not Lindsey Lohan. If you are the type that is always losing things look for a less expensive pair of shades from *Forever 21* or *Kohl's*. For those that have tried designer sunglasses and are never going back, drop by your local *Sunglass Hut* and try out the latest frames from *Ray Ban, Paul Smith,* and *Tory Burch.*

Funky eyeglasses - If you are one of the lucky ones to need prescription eyewear, now is the time to update your glasses and get a new set of frames. There will be days as a new mommy when you would rather stick your head in the diaper pail than stick your finger in your tired eyes to insert contact lenses. Having an updated pair of glasses to wear on the days your contacts won't cut it is critical to your new mommy style. Plus a funky pair of frames can disguise tired eyes with loads of preppy or edgy style. Fabulous frames do not have to be expensive. Check out your local *Lens Crafters* and give your health insurance provider a call to see if they will foot a portion of the bill.

Bling - A few sparkly pieces jazz up any outfit. Bling pulls attention away from areas you want to hide and refocuses it on places you want to flaunt. To show off a great collarbone, neckline, or cleavage, choose short necklaces. To pull attention to slender wrists or toned forearms, consider a cuff bracelet or loads of stacked bangles. A nice cocktail ring can jazz up a dressy outfit and make an everyday or work outfit feel a little bit more special. To avoid whiplash from tiny hands pulling at your sparkle avoid any extra-long jewelry around your neck or in your ears. Treat yourself to a few special pieces. Or leave this page open on daddy's pillow tonight as a subtle hint.

By making a few simple adjustments to your wardrobe you are helping to keep a bit of your stylish pre-baby self in your new mommy world. Not only will your new fashions keep you looking good, they will boost your confidence and help you feel great in your new role as a mom.

CHAPTER 2

Beauty

IN THE EARLY days of motherhood finding time for a beauty routine can feel as impossible as rocking your skinny jeans home from the hospital. However, this is no time to start neglecting yourself. If you do things can go downhill. Fast.

With a few quick tips you will look and feel great even amidst the crazy days of sleep deprivation. Fussy routines will become a thing of your past and simple regimens the way of your fabulous future.

Now is the time to toss the liquid liner, four step brow kits, and false lashes, and, in their place, stock up on a small handful of new mommy beauty essentials. These tools will keep you looking fresh and put together on the outside and beaming with confidence from within.

New Mommy Maintenance

As a new mom you won't have much time each day to accentuate your assets and cover up your flaws. Keeping up with your regular beauty maintenance is now more important than ever before. If the foundation of your look isn't up to snuff it will take extra effort and time (that you don't have!) to cover it up. Keep up with your mommy maintenance and you will look polished with minimal everyday effort.

Hair - The foundation of a great look is a terrific head of hair. Caring for your hair both at home and at the salon is the key to fabulous looking locks. To keep your style in tip-top shape, make a point to book professional maintenance every eight to twelve weeks.

A great hair style can be transformational. I was afraid to color my hair during pregnancy, so by the time the baby came my dark roots had grown out far past the point of acceptable. When my daughter was two weeks old, my mom visited and took care of her while I went to a styling appointment. I came back a nothing short of a new person. Finding the time to squeeze in salon visits will help keep your hair style and spirits up.

Managing your tresses at home can be a bit tougher now that you have a little one in tow. As silly as it sounds, you must intentionally carve out time to take a shower and wash your hair. Try shampooing in the evenings after baby is asleep or strap your honey into his bouncy chair right outside the shower and grab a quick wash in the A.M. Once a week make an appointment with yourself to deep condition your hair. Try to do it at the same time every week so you get used to the routine. Perhaps every Tuesday while your husband is giving the baby a bath.

Nails - Now is not the time in your life for long colorful nails. Short and sassy is your new signature look. Show off your style by keeping your nails neatly trimmed and topped with clear glossy polish. If you are doing your nails at home, try a couple coats from *Sally Hansen's Diamond Shine* polish collection. If professional manicures are something you enjoyed pre-baby, try to pop into the nail salon on a semi-regular basis for a touch up. Every two months will do the trick. Some salons are so quick and efficient you may even be able to bring baby with you during a quick cat nap in her car seat. At the salon look for *OPI Passion* – a subtly elegant, can't fail new-mommy color choice.

Teeth - Nothing spoils a great look like a set of icky yellow teeth. Luckily, you don't have to give up coffee or spend hours at the dentist to get your chiclets pearly white. Just make sure you brush regularly and pick up a box of *Whitestrips*. These magical strips are widely available at drug stores and extremely effective. For less than a mani/pedi you will have your smile back to sparkling white in about a week. Most strips are applied for less than thirty minutes a day and do not interfere with talking or even drinking water, making them ideal for your busy on-the-go new mommy lifestyle.

Eyebrows - Well-groomed eyebrows are like food and shelter to a beauty-ista. Your look simply can't survive without them! A well-maintained set of brows can accentuate modest cheekbones, make a wide face appear thinner, and open up the eyes to make you appear brighter and more awake (hallelujah). Invest in your brows by employing a professional. A brow waxing or tweezing takes less than 10 minutes and costs about as much as lunch out, making it an affordable and convenient luxury that doesn't even require a babysitter. Getting your brows done even once every two or three months will help them grow into their ideal shape. You just need to gently maintain them with a set of tweezers in between appointments. Touch up as needed with a soft pencil or a pressed powder like *Anastasia Eye Powder* applied with a sharp angled brush.

I took my daughter with me the first time I tried eyebrow threading. If you've never heard of threading it's worth a quick Google. On the plus side, the session was even faster than a tweezing or waxing, but

I was such a wimp the pain made my eyes tear and my body wince in agony. My poor daughter thought her mother was being tortured and screamed out in protest. Good thing it only lasted a few moments.

Face - Nothing ruins a flawless face like a poor complexion. Keep your skin glowing by following the new mommy golden rule: Thou shalt never go to bed with make-up on. Wash your face every night using a mild cleanser. Both *Ponds* and *Olay* have super convenient single-use cleansing towelettes that make make-up removal a breeze. Or try *L'Oreal's Go 360 Clean* all-in-one face wash. It comes with a handy scrublet that sticks to your shower wall eliminating the need for a washcloth. Follow up with a light moisturizer like *Neutrogena's Healthy Skin Lotion* or take a page out of your baby's book and smooth a dollop of *Eucerin Crème* into just-washed skin. No matter how tired you are at the end of the day, invest the three minutes it takes to properly wash your face.

Skin - As for the skin on the rest of your body keep it soft and smooth by using a moisturizing body scrub in the shower like *Olay Ribbons* or *Dove's deep moisture.* You can even use it to shave your legs. Follow up with a rich body cream and rub it in all over focusing on your elbows, knees, and feet. If you crave a little color, in lieu of skin-aging sunshine, opt for self-tanner. Avoid reincarnation as Snooki's long-lost sister by choosing a shade only slightly darker than your natural skin color. Apply thin layers until you achieve your desired color. If you don't yet have a favorite self-tanner, *Lancôme* makes a terrific flash bronzer for legs, face, and body.

Reduce stress - Carve out a few moments each day to take several deep cleansing breaths. Simply observing yourself breathing in and out will help calm and focus your mind. A more relaxed inner self will reflect as a more relaxed, more radiant outer self. A lavender flax eye pillow is a great prop to help chill your mind and soothe your tired eyes. The soft scent calms the inner spirit while the flax helps reduce puffiness. I am forever grateful to the mommy in my child birth education class for introducing me to the eye pillow. Even using it for two minutes a day will help. Pure new mommy bliss.

Easy Everyday Make-up

Create maximum impact with minimal make-up. Taking just five minutes each morning to apply a limited amount of makeup will help you shine throughout the day.

As my daughter got older she started taking an interest in watching mommy doing her make-up. Now I take special time with her plopped on my lap each morning as I sit on the floor and put on my face. Gosh, I hope I'm not creating the next *Toddler in Tiara*.

A quick application is all it takes to boost your new mommy confidence and create a pulled together look. For special occasions add a few extra steps to take pulled together to fab-u-losity and remind your hubby that he scored one hot mama.

Flawless face in five minutes (or less!)

Eye brightening crème - The most essential part of the new mommy make-up routine is creating big bright eyes. Behold the mac daddy and crown jewel of all eye products, eye brightening crème. This fabulous potion lightens delicate skin pigment and adds just a touch of shimmer to give the illusion of rested fresh skin. Apply liberally around the immediate eye area paying special attention to the inner corners and along the lash line. Check out *Olay Total Effect Eye Transforming Cream* or *Belli's Eye Brightening Cream.*

White eyeliner - Yes white eyeliner. A.K.A. mommy's magic stick. Use this in the inner corners of your eyes dangerously close to the lash line. Eyes instantly appear bigger, brighter, and more alert. Check out *Paula Dorf's Enhancer* eye liner. Inspired by her nephew's beautiful eyes, the pencil brightens the lower rim of the eye and can even double up as soft lip liner for a delicate pretty pout.

<u>*Cream-colored eye shadow*</u> - The right shade of cream shadow subtly lightens the face and brightens the eyes. Select a shade in the lightest possible beige, being careful not to choose anything too white. The best powder shadows are creamy and matte and do not flake when applied. Sweep a liberal amount over the lid and gently blend along the lash and brow line. Try *Clinique's* shadow in *French Vanilla* or *Bobby Brown's Cream Shadow Stick.*

<u>*Tinted moisturizer*</u> - Select a shade as close to your natural coloring as possible. Apply a thin layer all over the face to smooth out your complexion and nourish your skin. Using a make-up sponge or clean fingers, blend along the chin and hair line. *Cover Girl Smoothers* have been popular for eons for a reason. A quick sweep of this inexpensive-yet-luxurious cream and your skin will glow with balance and health.

<u>*Highlighter*</u> - A quick sweep of highlighter just above the cheekbones and in the brow arch is an easy way to instantly brighten the face and beautifully reflect light onto your skin. Look for a powder two shades lighter than your skin color with just a hint of

shimmer. *Benefit's High Beam* liquid highlighter and *Mac's powder white gold pigment* are two to try.

Bronzer - A quick sweep of bronzer adds a warm glow to tired skin. Apply just below the cheekbones, in the hollows of the face. After applying the bronzer it should look like you spent the afternoon in the outdoors and not at all like you are wearing make-up. The goal is sun-kissed not sun-torched. For a great liquid bronzer try *Origins Sunny Disposition Bronzer*. Or for a 2 in 1 product that is both a highlighter and a bronzer check out *NARS highlighting/ bronzing blush duo*.

Light sparkly lip gloss - Select your gloss in a muted shade close to your natural lip color. Blush, nude, or clear are wise options for most complexions. While the shade should be a subtle muted color, the finish should be high gloss with tons of sparkle and shine. By adding interest to your mouth with finish instead of color, you are creating a pulled together look that makes you gleam without looking too made up. Try *Lancôme's Juicy Tubes* in *Touched By Light* or *Pure*.

Flawless to fabulous (in just five more minutes!)

To add a little extra oomph to your look, invest five more minutes. These additional three steps will take your everyday face to a look more appropriate for evening or an extra special outing.

Mascara - Apply two coats of black mascara to your top and bottom lashes, focusing on the outer corners. Use a dry mascara wand to comb out clumps between coats and a damp *Q-tip* to remove any smudges on your skin. Eyes instantly appear more open and the dark framing adds extra polish to your fresh faced look. *Cover Girl Lash Blast* and *Maybelline Great Lash* are drugstore favorites. *Lancôme Fatale* and *Givenchy Phenomen'Eyes* are great department store picks to try.

Dark eye shadow - Transform your fresh bright eyes to va-va-voom in no time by applying a dark shade of eye shadow in the crease and outer corners. The color of eye shadow is up to you but aim for something deep enough to create contrast with the cream shadow on your lids. Green eyes look great with dark purple, blue eyes pop with chocolate brown, while both grey and brown eyes really come alive when nestled beside forest green. Lose yourself in a sea of amazing options at the *MAC* counter in *Nordstrom*.

Deep berry gloss - To make your mouth really pop, swap out your muted neutral gloss for a more stand out color. Choose a shade that best compliments your complexion. In general, the fairer your skin the more likely a shade in the pink family will work for you. Women with darker pigmentation can experiment with shades from the red, violet, or even brown families. Again look for something with a high gloss finish to pull together your posh and polished hot mama face. For a perfect combination of deep and delicious, try *Clinique's Superbalm Gloss* in *Currant* or *Raspberry*.

Easy Everyday Hair

Before you go chopping off your long locks into a short 'low-maintenance' mommy do consider this - short hair styles are often actually MORE maintenance than longer styles. Not only do they need more frequent trimming and upkeep at the salon, they can take much longer to get just right at home. They also completely take away your option to sweep uncooperative hair into a sleek effortless ponytail when you are in a pinch.

Obviously, I am totally jealous of any woman that can pull off a short haircut and still look fabulous. If you fall into this lucky category, you are probably super fit, effortlessly gorgeous, and not in need of hair advice, so feel free to skip ahead and meet back up with us in Chapter 3. For the rest of us longer-haired ladies read on for a few easy new mommy hair styles that will have you looking marvelous in a matter of minutes.

Hot Hair (in an instant)

Messy bun - The key to this style is for it to look effortlessly messy, even though it takes a wee bit of effort. This look is best for mommies with bangs or shorter pieces of hair in the front. 1) Sweep hair back into a loose low ponytail. 2) Twist the pony and then swirl it in a circle around the elastic until you run out of hair. 3) Secure with an elastic band ideally the same shades as your locks. Some pieces will stick out of the bun and that is okay, this is part of its messy charm. 4) Pull a few pieces of hair or bang out from the front to add a few face framing layers.

Pony with a twist - This small twist gives your boring ponytail hip chic style. This is a great option those of us with babies that have curious fingers and love to grab (read: yank) hair. 1) Sweep brushed hair tightly up into a traditional ponytail and secure with an elastic band. 2) Take a thin piece of hair from the ponytail approximately a half inch thick and wrap it around the elastic band. 3) Secure this stray piece of hair with a small clip or bobby pin directly underneath your ponytail so that it is barely visible. You can vary the height of your pony for a slight variation to this look.

Of all hair styles this is by far my favorite. It is so easy and it never fails to get at least one compliment. For some reason, if they can't see a visible elastic in your ponytail, people assume you've done something really complicated to create this beautiful, sophisticated look. I won't tell if you won't!

Beachy waves - If you are a mommy who squeezes in hair washings in the evening this look is for you. 1) Take damp hair and tie it in a loose bun at the nape of your neck. 2) When you wake up in the morning undo the bun and apply a dime sized amount of hair balm like *Fekkai Texturizing Balm*. 3) Scrunch with your hands and finish with medium hold hair spray.

Pinny head - This look is great with unwashed hair or beachy waves (see above). 1) Take a small strand of hair from the front, twist, and secure it about three inches from the hair line with a mini barrette or bobby pin. 2) Repeat with four or five strands randomly placed around the crown of your head. Do not select strands such that they are equidistantly placed around your head. For the best results, strands should overlap and appear randomly scattered throughout your hair.

Messy braid - To avoid looking '16 and Pregnant' only attempt this look if you have very long hair, ideally below your shoulder blades. 1) Loosely braid tresses together down the middle of your back. Begin to tighten the braids as you get closer to the end. 2) Secure with a clear mini elastic. 3) For extra style points and added maturity, top with a funky hat.

Even Hotter hair (in an instant plus a moment)

To take your look from every day to extra special spend just a few extra minutes primping with these great new mommy hair dress up tips.

Edgy pony - Take your sleek pony to the next level with this funky style. 1) Grab a 3 inch section of hair from your bangs (or where your bangs would be if you have grown yours out). 2) Secure the ponytail without this section of hair included. 3) Lightly tease your bangs, and then lay them on top of your head creating a ½ - 1½-inch bubble. 4) Secure the swoop with a clip or bobby pin, then wrap any extra length around your pony and fasten with a bobby pin.

Add some sparkle - In place of boring bobby pins or neutral elastics opt for a little hair bling. Look for jeweled hair ties, sparkly clips, skinny headbands, or barrettes with faux stones to add a little something special to your do. *Anthropologie* makes fantastic hair accessories, as do more affordable brands like *Goodie* and *Scunci*.

Quick curls - To get ready for a night on the town, amp up the volume with some curls. 1) Pop a half dozen large Velcro rollers into your hair and coat with spray gel. 2) Go about your business for 30-60 minutes. 3) Grab the blow dryer and quickly warm hair for a minute or so. 4) Gently remove rollers and generously spray with firm hold hair spray like *John Frieda's Frizz Easy Firm Hold Spray*.

Time Saving Tips & Tricks

Bundle your beauty - Scanning through all the mommy maintenance you aspire to do can feel overwhelming. When is a busy new mom able to find time to get all this accomplished? Instead of treating each element like an individual task bundle multiple tasks together and get them all done at the same time. For example allocate the first 20 minutes of your baby's Monday morning nap to mommy maintenance. Apply a whitestrip to your teeth and jump in a hot shower. Spend the first ten minutes deep conditioning your hair, the next five tweezing stray brows and filing unruly nails, and the final five applying and drying a coat of glossy clear nail polish.

I tried this bundling idea without much success over the first few weeks of my daughter's life. More than once I ended up getting out of the shower soaking wet, hair still dripping with deep conditioner, trying to nurse a screaming infant. But over time, as we established more of a routine, I found this to be a really effective way to accomplish a large number of tasks in a short period of time. As a bonus, it was also a nice indulgence for me to feel like I was spending some time prioritizing myself.

Schedule schedule schedule - Get on your stylist's schedule now. Pre-book six months or even a year's worth of appointments to ensure you will make it to the salon for your maintenance on a regular basis. Putting your commitments on the calendar will keep you more accountable for showing up. Having your appointments scheduled far in advance will also help you find someone to watch your munchkin while you bliss out at your blow out.

Online shopping - Embrace the world of online beauty care. With a quick click of your mouse, you can ensure you never run out of any of your new mommy beauty essentials ever again. Some sites like *Drugstore.com* and *Amazon.com* even let you set up your purchases on auto-replenishment, meaning you can have your products delivered every one, three, or six months depending on how frequently you tend to run out. Can you say e-z?

Dry shampoo - I can't say enough wonderful things about dry shampoo. On the days that you simply can't squeeze in a shower this miracle-in-a-can keeps this stinky fact a secret between just you and your shower. Not only does dry shampoo evaporate dirt and oil, it also adds a fresh scent and oodles of volume. In fact, celebrities often use dry shampoo to give extra oomph to their voluminous styles on the red carpet. In a pinch, baby powder has a similar effect to dry shampoo and has the added bonus of being abundantly available in most new mommy households. Just make sure to adequately rub in the powder to ensure the white color does not make your roots appear grey.

Vaseline - I love Vaseline and carry it with me everywhere I go. Seriously. I really, really love it. Vaseline is an excellent remedy for dry hands, the absolute cheapest (and surprisingly pretty) lip balm on the planet, and a fantastic moisturizer for baby's skin. Purchase the mini tub, not the tube. For some reason the tub as a thicker, more luxurious consistency. Throw it in your jacket pocket, purse, or diaper bag. You never know when it will come in handy, for you or your baby.

Frownies - If your little one's funny antics have you furrowing your brow more often than your dermatologist would like, Frownies are for you. These magic pads adhere to your skin for a few hours, ideally while you sleep, and miraculously erase the creases between your eyes and on your forehead. They are totally chemical-free and a great option for new mommies who want to freshen up their look but are way too young (and savvy) for scary surgical procedures. The only downside of this product is that they look hideous when you put them on, so use them when you are home alone or on the nights you really aren't in the mood and want a way to throw a subtle, but effective hint to your partner.

As a new mom, there never seems to be enough time. Try to avoid using time as the excuse to deprioritize your beauty routine. You always find ten extra minutes to clean the crib sheets when you are met with a soaked surprise in the morning. Try to find the same extra time for yourself. With the right tools and tricks, even a few minutes can make a big difference.

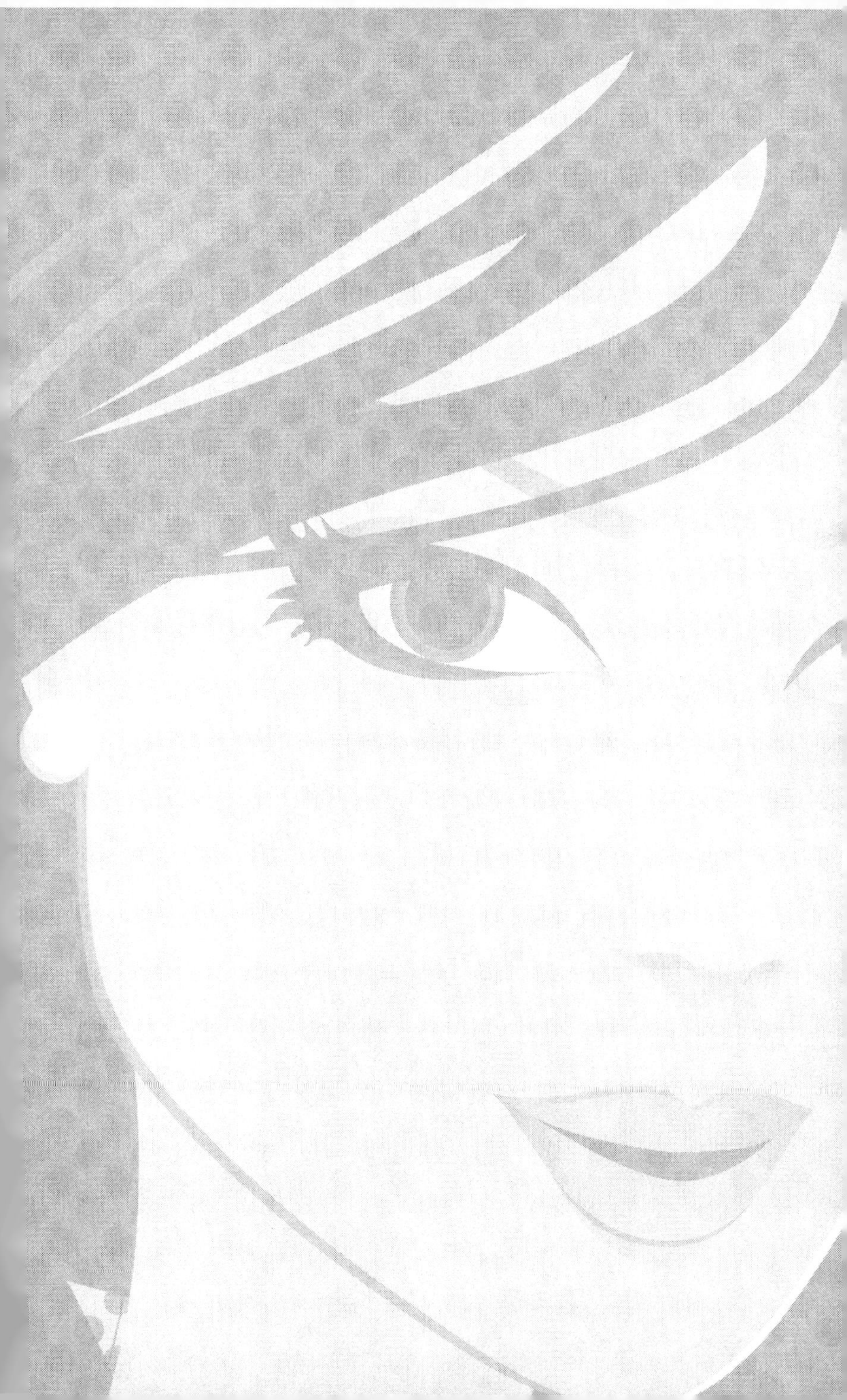

CHAPTER 3

Home Décor

AFRAID YOUR HOME is about to resemble the local *Gymboree*? If you're terrified by the thought of your chic modern pad becoming littered with loud toys and diaper pails, read on.

Your home is your sanctuary and you must treat it as such. Having a comfortable place where you can relax and unwind is a critical part of becoming the calm, peaceful, happy mommy you want to be. This is especially important now that you will be spending more time there. You want a space that you love living in. You should find it both inspiring and rejuvenating.

Of course you want your home to be baby-friendly, just remember that does not mean that your baby must become the center of your decorating scheme! With a few clever tips, you can have a baby-friendly home that both your little one and your grownup friends will adore equally.

Begin by defining which spaces in your home will be used to primarily to entertain family, baby, or adults-only. Then set up each room according to that purpose. Organizing your house this way will keep the primary-colored chaos in its place and add a sense of calmness and order to your life.

Family Zone

The family zone exists in the spaces where you spend most of your time. This is where you and your baby will spend your days playing, babbling, and cuddling up a storm. It will likely comprise the majority of your home. To select which rooms should be part of the family zone, think about the areas in your home that you use the most. For most families, this includes the kitchen, living/dining/family room, and primary bathroom. In this zone, you will mesh your new baby gear with your stylish pre-baby décor.

Add Storage

If there is one thing that every family zone needs, it's storage. Look to add storage throughout the family zone wherever possible. More is better. Less is worse.

Add storage to existing pieces - If you don't want to buy new items, instead look for ways to add storage to things you already have. For example, can you add doors to your open cabinetry or throw a chic piece of fabric over an exposed end table? Can you make your existing closets work harder for you? Custom closet organizers, like *California Closets*, can go a long way in controlling clutter. For a less expensive option, check out do-it-yourself closet organization systems available at retailers like *IKEA*.

Load up on bins and baskets - Storage baskets today are surprisingly stylish. Available in a wide variety of colors and finishes, bins and baskets do a great job hiding small odds and ends. Bins with lids are extra fabulous as they keep your mini-clutter totally out of sight and therefore out of mind. You can find storage baskets in different shapes and sizes to accommodate most any place you would want to put them. You can store your baskets in open cabinetry, on deep wall shelves, on the second tier of a coffee table, atop a desk, or even tucked behind a large house plant or couch. Storage baskets are especially helpful in the bathroom. These bins can keep your baby's lotions, shampoo, washcloths, and hooded towels easily accessible and stylishly stowed. For an ultra-polished look, roll up towels and washcloths before placing them in the bins. Stylish baskets are easy to find at national retailers like *The Container Store, HomeGoods*, and *Target*.

I went a little crazy on bins and baskets. In fact, I love them so much I actually have a small closet full of empty containers just waiting for more baby things to fill them up. Who knew baskets could hold so much? I truly thought I would need twice as many as I did. In retrospect, I think it would be a good idea to calculate how many baskets you really need before making the purchase.

Buy a stylish trunk - Check out a vintage home goods store or flea market to find the queen bee of all storage bins, the antique chest. A chest is a stylish addition to any home and goes with almost any décor. In addition to bringing oodles of funky style, trunks and chests hold an incredible amount of anything. Equivalent to the modern day suitcase, trunks were designed for the rich and privileged to bring all of their luxe goods with them during periods of lengthy travel. Your baby's clutter is no match for the awesome antique chest.

Explore New Furniture

Beyond storage, there is never a better excuse to invest in some new furniture than after the birth of your first baby. When deciding which pieces to update, first look for opportunities to increase your storage potential, by replacing old furniture. Can you swap the table in your entranceway for a small dresser with drawers? Exchange the bench at the foot of your bed for a version that includes storage? A few new items will not only update your décor and increase your storage capacity, but they can also make your home easier maintain and safer for your baby. If your budget is tight, check out vintage or second hand stores for your new pieces. Also, remember to donate your old stuff for a tax deduction. For inspiration, consider these surprisingly sleek and baby-friendly options.

Coffee table - In lieu of a traditional coffee table, place two rectangular tufted ottomans side-by-side. These pieces have soft corners and look so much sleeker than adding ugly foam corners to your stylish, but dangerous, wood or glass table. Top with a large serving tray and you can easily dress up the table with flowers, candles, and pictures when entertaining. The solid surface also doubles as an everyday table that can hold a box of crayons, snack tray, or dinner plate.

End table - Consider using a soft suede storage cube as an end table. The cube looks smart and can easily double as a footrest or extra seat if you have guests. Most importantly, like the storage ottoman it is baby friendly with its soft edges and round corners, plus it boasts extra storage inside.

Headboard - Instead of a heavy iron or wood headboard in your bedroom, look for a cushy option wrapped in fabric. Soft tufted headboards are more comfortable for reading and lounging in bed. (And they hurt less if a rowdy night leads to a bump on the head, but that is another book…). Most importantly, they create an inviting place for baby and keep him safe while cruising around with mommy and daddy in bed.

Desk - If you don't use your office desk daily consider installing a desk alternative. Instead of a traditional version with hard legs and sharp corners install a simple 18-inch wood plank against your wall and secure with fancy brackets. The 'desk' should reach far enough out from the wall to accommodate tucking in your chair and provide a sturdy solid surface for you to work on. For the extra paranoid, round the edges and/or install the plank at bar height to make it extra tough for your baby to get into trouble.

Dining table - Most dining room or kitchen tables are full of sharp corners that give baby plenty of opportunities to get into trouble. Consider purchasing a round table supported by a sturdy pillar instead of traditional legs. Not only do circular tables facilitate great conversation, they also minimize the need to baby proof the corners. Opt for wood over glass unless you like the way little handprints look smudged all over your table.

Accessories

Accessorizing is the key to great home design. Did you know that many chic accessories can double as fun and safe toys for your baby? Check out these clever décor elements that won't add an ounce of primary colored clutter.

Decorative balls - A bowl of decorative balls adds style to any flat surface and doubles as a toy that can entertain a baby for hours. Well, minutes. I don't know of anything that amuses a baby for hours. Balls are available in many sizes and colors to coordinate with any décor. Look for materials that will mesh with your style and are interesting and safe for baby to explore. Select balls that are at least as big as an apple. Avoid anything covered with potential choking hazards like feathers, buttons, or pebbles. Your baby will love to touch and feel the different textures and enjoy rolling the balls on the floor. Once he is finished playing simply return the balls to the bowl and voilà! You have eliminated toy clutter and added style points back into your room. I have amazing pictures of my daughter sitting in a large bowl of decorative balls laughing and playing. Priceless.

Ceiling fan - Young babies are especially obsessed with ceiling fans. Consider installing a stylish fan or two in lieu of a traditional light fixture to keep rooms cool and give your infant something to look at. Avoid ceiling fans in rooms that you want baby to sleep in. Once he notices the magical fan it may be hard for him to concentrate on anything else, including sleep!

Black and white photographs - Babies do not obtain full vision until around eight months old. Until then, many are mesmerized by black and white patterns. Instead of investing in black and white flashcards or toys, frame some black and white pictures. Considering using photos of your family. You can use these as tools to familiarize him with family members, especially those that you don't get to see very often. When my daughter was a few months old she loved to stare, giggle, and point at black and white photos from our wedding. I loved to see the amusement on her face and was equally pleased that she was sharing in special moments between her Dad and me.

Clear shower curtain - Swap your existing shower curtain for a crisp, clear, see-through version. A clear curtain will make your bathroom appear bigger and, more importantly, make it much easier for you to grab a shower. The clear curtain (or glass door) lets you keep one eye on baby while you suds up in the shower.

Baby Zone

No new mama's house would be complete without a baby zone. Unlike the family zone, where you are trying to gently infuse baby into your décor, the baby zone is designed with baby at the center.

The baby zone should include at least one room dedicated, and decorated, just for baby. For most families the baby zone is comprised of a nursery and a playroom. The one rule with the baby zone is that you should locate it somewhere behind closed doors. This area of your home is the one that from time to time will look like it was hit by hurricane-5-month-old, so it is nice to have the option to simply close the door when you need to.

If your home affords the space for a dedicated playroom, take advantage of this luxury. This room might not get a ton of use at the beginning of baby's life but it will become more and more important as he, and his toy collection, grows. A playroom is the perfect place to store anything baby that you don't care to look at on a daily basis. You will appreciate this when your pumpkin decides her favorite play things is the bright green and yellow talking caterpillar instead of the adorable handmade soft pink and white painted wooden train that you splurged on when you were pregnant.

When designing this zone, keep in mind that just because this is your baby's space you don't have to totally sacrifice style. These clever baby décor tips will help create a space that both you and baby will love.

Nursery

<u>*Get outside the baby stores*</u> - While it is tempting and easy to simply order a matching set of baby furniture and linens from your favorite national baby retailer, super savvy mommies know that this is only one of your many options. Baby décor does not have to come from a baby store! Scour your favorite shops to look for pieces that you love and that fit with your nursery décor and color scheme. Your dresser might be *Crate & Barrel,* your shelving *IKEA,* and your rug *West Elm.* Mixing and matching complementary items is a great way to up your nursery's style and acquire some new pieces that might get a second life outside the nursery as baby grows up.

<u>*Lose the cutesy baby bed in a bag*</u> - The fabrics and accessories you select for your nursery do not all have to be within a matching butterfly, car, or giraffe theme. If a more sophisticated nursery is

more your style select accessories and fabrics within a baby friendly color theme that you love. For example, soft pink, frosted mint, and white for a girl; ocean blue, buttercream, and khaki for a boy. Select bedding, lamps, rugs, art, window treatments, and whatever else you fancy, within this color pallet. Mixing and matching grown-up and baby patterns like plaids, solids, hearts, and polka dots within your color pallet will make your room feel cozy, full of texture, and very pulled together.

I didn't figure this out until I had looked through literally hundreds of baby bedding options from every store and website I could find. As I scrolled through page after page of Princess, Dora, and bunny blankets with matching drapes, lamps, and rugs, I felt totally discouraged. The light bulb went off when I realized newborns don't sleep with blankets. I picked up a few inexpensive sheets and a neutral crib skirt instead. Then I accented the bedding with fun, sophisticated curtains, lamps, and rugs in baby friend colors.

Personalize - Black and white photography is a great way to add chic personalization to any nursery décor. You can frame baby photos, early ultrasound pictures, or even a montage of your pregnant belly. If you enjoy recording your baby's milestones in his baby book, consider creating a large calendar on the nursery wall to track and celebrate milestones as they occur. Think about things that are important to your family and incorporate them into the room.

For example if your family loves animals, a zoo theme may be the perfect fit for your home. If you are world travellers, maybe a globally inspired décor would be ideal for your family.

Look for dual purpose items - When furnishing the nursery it is tempting to go over the top decorating to create the ultimate adorable cozy space for your little one. However, unless you plan on having more than a handful of children, most of the furnishings will be quickly outgrown and discarded. For this reason, look for items that can serve more than one purpose over time, especially if they are expensive. For example, you may be better off purchasing a super comfy reclining glider in a neutral fabric instead of a cheap padded rocking chair in baby pink if, after you are finished using it for nursing, you can re-purpose the chair as your husband's new favorite place to watch the game. Likewise, a cherry wood dresser with large drawers has a better chance at a second life than a similar model with teeny cupboards in soft powder blue.

Disguise the cheap - For items that you know will have a brief shelf life, but you just can't resist, look for less expensive versions and dress them up with cute accessories. For example adding new hardware can jazz up an inexpensive dresser. There are oodles of adorable baby-friendly drawer pulls available to match almost any dresser and décor. I especially love the collection at *Anthropologie*. Similarly, a modest crib can be easily dressed up with a chic mobile and a set of bright new sheets, just as a bare wall can take on new life when accented with framed pages of your favorite Dr. Seuss books. *P.S. Dr. Seuss' The Lorax has a fabulous message that is worth reading to your precious little one.*

Playroom

Toy storage - Pick up a set of fabric toy bins. Use them to sort toys in categories that make sense to you. One clever mommy might choose to sort them by baby age, while another might feel it makes more sense to sort by toy type i.e. rattles, blocks etc. Do what works for you and makes you feel organized in your own mind. Add adorable labels to up the style quotient and make finding things a snap. Store your fabric toy bins in a shelving unit to minimize clutter and allow you to control the pace at which you introduce toys to baby.

Soft, inexpensive flooring - Avoid expensive carpet in the playroom. This space is intended to be fun and is where your little one will explore crayons, chalk, and finger painting. The floor is bound to get dirty! Since your little one will spend time in here before mastering the delicate art of toddling, you'll also want a soft place for him to cruise and explore. Not to mention a comfy surface for you to sit while you are playing with him. Look for a plush, chic, inexpensive room-sized floor rug. For extra comfort and safety place a large rug pad underneath. If your room does happen to be carpeted don't dismay, just prepare to shell out a little extra cash for professional carpet cleaning when the need arises, or just throw a cheap coordinating area rug right on top.

Creativity corner - Consider dedicating a section of the playroom for baby to visually express himself through art. At around 6-9 months old, you can start introducing this area to your little one. Initially this space may only be used for simple finger painting with rice cereal and mashed up squash. For older children, the creativity corner might include an easel and a drawing desk. If you have the space, try covering one or two walls in white paper and letting your baby loose with the crayons and markers. For the more daring, you could cover the wall in chalkboard paint and let your baby mark it up with chalk art. While your baby is too small to use the chalkboard himself, you can use it to scribble love notes to him or record important milestones.

Educational wall art - Providing a stimulating learning environment does not have to mean swapping your trendy playroom for a drab classroom. With a little creativity you can cleverly infuse learning cues into your décor. For example, to help with reading and writing skills, hang A-Z wooden letters in a funky font on the wall. To explain numbers, install a magnetic board with a fabulous frame and place number magnets on it in numerical order. To advance your little one's grasp of measurement, put a growth chart on one wall that extends up to the ceiling. Not only can you show your little one how tall she is getting, you can also explain how tall the room is and how the two compare. To explain time, place a funky clock in the room. To teach geography, post an erasable map on the wall. Let your imagination be your only limit to finding clever ways to infuse learning time into playtime.

Adult-only Zone

Every home needs an adult-only zone. Well at least my home needs one. After a few weeks of seeing baby things around every corner, I started to go a bit batty. I cleared off the tub area so that I could have a toy-free soak. It was so enjoyable I realized that I needed a larger baby-free space that I could escape to from time to time.

Declare at least one area in your home where no baby things are allowed. This is a place that is free of loud sing-a-long toys, diapers, and baby proofing. You can retreat to the adult-only zone at any time when you need a break. This is YOUR space.

Make a point to keep baby out of this zone as much as possible.

You can use this space to relax, reconnect with your spouse, take a five-minute time-out, or re-gain your sanity after a particularly trying day or night. Some days you may use the adult-only zone to veg while your baby is napping. Other days you may use it to take a few deep breaths to calm yourself after trying to calm an inconsolable baby.

Try to keep this area neat and tidy so that it truly feels like an escape and not a space that reminds you of the household chores that you could be doing. Regardless of which room(s) you choose, spending time in this zone should help you to feel more relaxed, refreshed, and a little more like YOU! Make a point to spend time in your adult zone every day, even if it is just five minutes.

Of course, the funny thing about the adult-only zone is when you spend time in it, you'll probably start missing your little one. No matter how relaxed I get in my clutter-free, toy-free bliss after my daughter goes to bed, I find I start missing her kissable cheeks about an hour later. I got into a terrible habit of going into her room when the pang got too strong, picking her up and cuddling her. Let's just say it's true what they say. Never wake a sleeping baby.

Couple time - For some pairs the adult-only zone can be a great place to spend time with your spouse while the baby is sleeping. If the primary use of your adult-only zone will be couple time, choose a place that reminds you of the connection you shared even before the baby was born. For example, if the two of you are avid readers and spent a good portion of your courtship cuddled up reading together, your library or office would be a good choice for your adult-only zone. If you want this zone to be a more intimate place that helps put the sizzle back in your saddle you might even make your bedroom part of the adult only zone. Keeping your eyes off the bouncy chair might help keep your mind on the romance. If you love having your little one with you in bed in the mornings compromise and make this room part of the family zone during the day, but adult-only after dark.

Individual time - Some couples like to have more than one room in the adult-only zone, especially if they are the type that enjoy spending alone time without their spouse. Daddy may declare the basement workshop or garage part of his adult-only zone while mom selects the bathroom, with the fabulous window seat and phenomenal soaker tub, as her adult-only space. Finding areas of the house where each of you can relax separately is a great way to refresh yourself or blow off some steam during a disagreement. (You can make up later with some extra couple time).

Thinking time - One important role of the adult-only zone is that it should be a place where you can come to reconnect with the pre-baby you. Use it as a place to think about the things that you truly enjoyed doing before the baby was born, and make a plan for how to incorporate the most important things back into your post-baby life. For example if you and your husband used to enjoy running as a couple, consider purchasing a jogging stroller so you can go on a nice leisurely run together. If you used to enjoy painting, schedule a painting session with yourself on the first Monday of every month during one of baby's naps. If you miss working out, start researching gyms in your area that offer child care. Finding ways to carve out time for you is the foundation of becoming the happy mommy you want to be and the strong woman that is able to give your baby the very best of you every day.

Entertaining

There is nothing scarier for new parents than entertaining, especially if your guests don't have babies. At least other parents understand why your house can look like a daycare even though you only have ten pounds of baby living with you. Here are a few ideas to knock the style socks of your guests and leave them wondering how you do it all.

Keep entertaining within the family zone - You have enough to do preparing for company without having to clean up the entire house. Lucky for you the rooms in the baby zone have doors. Just close them! Quickly tidy the family zone using your hidden storage bins, baskets, and ottomans to toss any stray toys or clutter.

Light some candles - The absolute number one way to create a polished looking pad is with a little candlelight. For some reason glowing candles give the illusion that you are so organized you actually have spare time to light candles. In reality, it takes only about ninety seconds to set your home aglow. Light a few tea lights in the bathroom, a pillar candle in the dining room, and a few warmly scented sticks throughout you living area. In fact, don't save candlelight for entertaining only and spark a few up any evening. Light a few candles before your husband gets home from work. You'll have him thinking motherhood transformed his wife into a domestic goddess. Not to mention how great you will look in the candlelight. Just be cautious to keep candles out of baby's reach and never leave them unattended.

Pick up fresh flowers - Flowers brighten up any space and are a fabulous addition to every décor. Grab a bunch on your regular trip to the grocery store or farmer's market. Place the flowers in a vase, mason jar, or wine decanter. If you are going to have flowers on the dinner table, cut them short to avoid them interfering with your conversation. Short bouquets look best if the vase is very full so pack your blooms in tight. Another über-stylish option is to remove all the leaves from the stems, tie the flowers together with a neutral colored twist tie, and lean the tied bouquet against the side of the vase.

Smile - When your guests compliment your home and comment how incredible it is that you keep things so together even with a baby, just smile and accept the complement. Sure you are implying that your home always looks like this, but who are you to destroy their fantasy that it is possible to do it all, even with a baby? Keep the dream alive!

Keeping a chic home can be really tough after having a little one. But you can do it! Even focusing on just a few rooms can help keep your spirits up. You spend too much time in your home to not love living in it. It's not possible to avoid all the baby chaos all the time, but even the smallest adjustments will help keep your pad, and your mind, peaceful and clutter-free.

CHAPTER 4

Diet and Exercise

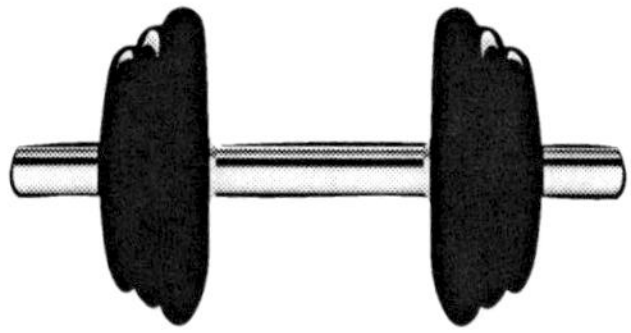

THIS IS THE chapter where I am supposed to tell you things like, "It took nine months to put it on, so don't worry if it takes nine months to take it off" or "Embrace your delicious new mommy curves." Well, I'm not going to. Getting your body back into fighting shape is an important part of the quest to claim your most stylish, magnificent life as a new mom. After all, even the best clothes lose their fabulousness if you can't fit them over your ass. Losing the baby weight will boost your confidence, help you cope with sleep deprivation, make you feel sexier, increase your energy, and encourage you to embrace the mommy goddess inside of you.

If you plan on taking nine months to lose all your baby weight, the likelihood is that you will lose interest around month five or six and that extra seven baby pounds will become yours for life. Let's face it; none of us stick with many things for nine whole months. If we'd had the choice even pregnancy would have been over around month seven or so.

I have yet to meet a real mommy who actually wants to celebrate or embrace her new 'curvy' body. Unfortunately, our post-baby curves often don't show up as voluptuous, Jessica Rabbit hips and a full, perky chest. More often we end up with a saggy tush, a set of dimply thighs, and a belly that jiggles like a bowl full of Christmas jelly. If you happen to be the one lucky woman whose body reinvents itself as Salma Hayek after childbirth, by all means, embrace your new sexy self. I am super-jealous of you and your newfound hotness. For the rest of us who want to banish the baby weight ASAP, read on for how to safely, but effectively, bring your hot body back – and maybe even make it better than ever.

Nutrition

For most women, the most effective way to decrease the overall size of the body is with proper nutrition. Knowing what to eat is usually not the hard part. You've read a million and one times that a diet of fresh fruits, vegetables, whole grains, low fat dairy, and lean meat trumps processed fast food, white bread, and sugar. You are well aware that for weight loss, 1500-2000 calories a day beats 3000-4000+. It's actually eating this way consistently that is the hard part!

Since you already know what you should be eating, I won't bore you with 101 'quick and nutritious' recipes or take up the next hour of your life with a lecture about fiber and fresh food. If you really are lost on what to eat or need ideas for healthy meals, spend a few minutes on *Google* or pick up a cookbook on healthy eating. Those authors are much better equipped to help you than I. To assist you with the hard part of sticking to your healthy eating plan here are a few tips to help you on your journey.

Water, water, water - Each morning fill up a half gallon milk jug. Your goal is to have consumed the whole thing by the end of the day. Reach for your water every time you want a snack, especially a sweet one. Often a glass of water will curb a craving by making you feel more full and giving your brain enough time to get your mind off the sugar. If you are not a big fan of plain water try adding some lemon, lime, orange, or cucumber slices. Increasing your water intake also helps improve your digestion and energy levels. This alone can be a game changer in your weight loss journey.

Banish fast food - Poof, it's gone. Just like you eventually will tell your baby that his pacifier no longer exists, now is the time for you to pretend fast food just disappeared. No more excuses. You are not pregnant anymore so you can't call it a 'craving'. Even though you can talk yourself into a thousand reasons why you deserve a fast food treat, you simply cannot have it while you are trying to lose your baby weight. Cutting out fast food will force you to create healthier habits. By replacing the meals you would have ordered up at the drive-thru with nutritious home cooking, you are fast tracking yourself to the body you want. Think of all the money you will save. You can spend the extra cash on new cute teeny tiny clothes, both for baby and for you! Once you reach your goal weight you can start slowly re-introducing an occasional fast food treat. But not until then. Period.

THINK: I am what I eat - Do you want to look like a doughy round cheese pizza or a crisp thin carrot? Even though you have heard it a thousand times never is this saying more true than after childbirth, especially if you are breastfeeding. Nursing mommies are the primary and often only source of nutrition for their little ones. You do not have to totally stress out about eating perfectly every single day to create milk that is nutritious for your baby. However, having a well-balanced and nutrient rich diet certainly isn't going to hurt. Your body is a temple, and the food you put in it an offering to the goddess within you. You wouldn't offer a Big Mac and a bag of donut holes to the gods would you? Then don't offer it to yourself either. Eat light fresh foods and you will feel light and fresh. Eat heavy greasy meals and you will feel heavy and greasy. It really is that simple.

Weigh yourself every day - It's harsh. I know. I don't recommend doing this forever, but for the time between delivery and when you reach your goal weight it can be a useful tool. Scales don't lie. The number staring back at you will help keep you honest as you progress through your weight loss journey. As the weeks and months go on you may start to get used to your bigger self and feel that you look good enough, especially compared to right after the birth. This thinking can be especially prevalent if you gained weight fairly proportionally all over your body. It will be harder to notice a thicker waist if it is nicely in proportion to your (also wider) hips. The scale will keep you in check. If you are eating well and exercising regularly, you *will* lose the weight. The scale will become a tool that shows you the fabulous progress you are making. It will become more inspiring and less frightening with every passing day.

Have someone else make your meals - If you can afford it, consider a healthy food delivery service. It may seem expensive but think about how much money you spend every month on take-out or your shoe collection. Can you prioritize your health above one of these things at least for a few months? Another more affordable option is to go to a place like *Let's Dish* where you prepare a month's worth of healthy food in one afternoon and then freeze it until it is time to eat. If your husband is looking for a way to help out ask him to take the reins in the kitchen. If birthing triplets feels like a better idea than eating your husband's cooking, instead ask him to take over the grocery shopping and keep the house stocked with healthy food and snacks. If friends or family members offer to help, ask them to prepare a healthy meal or two for you.

No sweets in the house - You can absolutely have sweets. Actually, you can have as many as you want. What is the catch? You can only eat sweets outside of your house. If you are really craving a cookie or an ice cream you have to go out and get it. Having to bundle your little munchkin up and leave the house will help you decide if you really want it or not. Often, especially if you walk to get your fix, you will find you won't really even want it once you get there. There is nothing wrong with indulging now and again. Just don't make it too easy for yourself by keeping a cupboard full of caramels and marshmallows.

Living down the street from a Dairy Queen was an amazing way for me to test this strategy. When I'd get bored mid-day and become focused on a Heath Blizzard fix, I'd strap on my baby carrier and start making my way to the DQ. I could not believe how many times I got there and opted to just keep on walking instead. After getting moving I just didn't feel the craving like I did when I was sitting around at home thinking about it.

Swap salad for soup - If you are anything like me the idea of eating cold salads every day is not very appealing. With all the chopping and mixing they can be tough to make with a little one on your hip. So leave the lettuce to the rabbits and stock up on soup instead. Soups are delicious, filling, and super quick to make. If you have an electric can opener you can probably even do it with one hand. Select soups with either a clear broth or a creamy vegetable puree base. Avoid anything cream or cheese based. Herbed tomato, butternut squash, and roasted red pepper are a few of my favorites. If you are adventurous you can even make your own. For a simple, classic soup, combine noodles (ideally whole grain) and vegetables with a ready-made broth. Or if you prefer a creamier texture, puree a few baked veggies and broth in a food processor. Heat and voilà!

One-handed snacks - Keep healthy snacks that are easy to grab and eat with one hand stocked in your kitchen at all times. Great options include apples, baby carrots, fruit leather, energy bars (I especially like *Lara, Cliff,* and *Kind*), raw almonds, pre-made smoothies, and berries. Soups can also qualify if you lose the spoon and store them in thermal mugs for easy sipping. One-handed snacks are great for the moments you are starving but not able to take a long enough break from your mommy duties to make a proper meal.

My girlfriend once told me about the first time she left her husband at home with the baby all day. She came home to a house littered with Power Bar wrappers, scattered on the floor among every baby toy and apparatus they owned. He explained he was starving but couldn't figure out how to make food while holding the baby. Hopefully you won't have to eat one-handed for breakfast, lunch and dinner like he did, but such snacks do come in handy from time to time when you are in a pinch.

No crash diets - Remember that post-baby weight loss is something that your body was designed to do. With proper nutrition and activity the weight will come off. You will be amazed at how quickly you can regain your pre-baby body. As a general guideline you can expect to lose the first 10-15 pounds the first week or so, then about a pound a week after that. That means if you gained an average amount of weight, 30-35 lbs., during your pregnancy you can expect to be rid of the excess in about four months. For those of us that spent the last nine months living on a few extra doughnuts and *Taco Bell*, the work will be a harder and take a little bit longer. But you don't need crash diets. In fact if you lose the weight this way it is bound to come back. You will not be able to keep up with this type of diet long term. Plus, crash diets will leave you feeling lethargic, cranky, and HUNGRY! I have yet to meet a fabulous hungry mommy. If you are nursing, crash diets can be especially dangerous. Significantly reducing your calorie intake can affect your milk supply and lead to problems with breast-feeding. Keep in mind that the weight loss process takes time. Even supermodels aren't back in their size 0's a week after they had a baby (no matter how good they look on their airbrushed magazine covers). Be patient with yourself. Be consistent and you *will* get the results you are after.

Take a multi-vitamin - No one has perfect nutrition every single day. Adding a multi-vitamin to your daily routine is a nice way to ensure you are getting all the necessary vitamins and minerals your body needs to keep it running in tip top shape. This is especially important for nursing mommies as well as for vegetarians or anyone on a restrictive diet like dairy- or gluten-free. Talk to your health care professional to help select the right vitamin supplement(s) for you.

Try on your bathing suit - Yikes. Every week or so try on an item of clothing you aspire to fit back into. It could be a bathing suit, skimpy dress, pair of jeans, or sexy piece of lingerie. This exercise will help give you a reality check as to where you are on your weight loss journey. Sometimes after a couple days of living in your comfy *Lululemon* pants, you will need to remind yourself there are other items of clothing in your wardrobe that you aspire to wear again someday. Trying on your goal outfit right as a chocolate chip craving strikes might also help keep the cookie monster at bay for at least a little while. The process may be painful the first few weeks, but you will feel so accomplished and amazing the first time you slip on that hot little number and it fits your oh-so-sexy-self just perfectly.

I was feeling pretty good about my shape shortly after childbirth. I didn't have the guts to slither into my teeniest bikini but I did try on a few lacey pieces that had always made me feel pretty good about myself pre-baby. This gave me a reality check that I had made good progress but wasn't quite ready to splurge on a Big Mac just yet. I used this little trick every time I felt like skipping a workout or cuddling up with a loaf of chocolate chip banana bread.

Repeat the hot mama mantra: NOTHING TASTES AS GOOD AS BEING THIN - I heard this on Oprah years ago. I love how this phrase makes you realize that your wellbeing is really in your hands. You can choose if you'd prefer to have dessert every night and five extra pounds, or no dessert and five less pounds. No matter how good that slice of chocolate cake looks you have to decide if it will look better on your hips or on the plate. Don't be afraid to indulge once in a while, one pig out won't make you look obscene. But a month's worth might. Think about how good you will feel once you reach your goal weight. Visualize yourself zipping your skinny jeans. Fill your mind with positive thoughts about how you will feel reaching your goal weight. Feel it. Smell it. Taste it. Soon it will be yours to savor.

Remember you are a role model now - Your baby is watching your every move from a very young age. It is never too early to start creating good habits. When your baby starts to mimic you, including your food habits, you will be glad you made the decision to role modeling healthy eating. Be careful not to treat food as 'scary' or 'an enemy'.

Show a healthy appreciation for good nutrition and eat high quality meals on a regular basis. The first time your baby reaches for a sweet, fresh raspberry over a store bought chocolate cookie you will feel so proud that you helped shape this choice by setting a great example.

Mix in a little vegetarian - A few nights each month, ideally once or twice a week, cook a meatless dinner. There is nothing wrong with having a reasonable amount of lean meat in your diet. I for one couldn't live without turkey dinner or a good filet mignon now and again. However, making a point to cook vegetarian meals will force a few extra vitamins into your diet and should reduce your overall intake of saturated fat. In general, vegetarian meals are higher in quality nutrients, lower in fat and cholesterol, and can be surprisingly filling. Try BBQ grilled portobello mushrooms, peppers, and zucchini glazed with balsamic vinegar and fresh herbs. Or make a thick and spicy vegetarian chili with a variety of hearty beans. Even my husband will eat these dinners, which is really saying something if you knew my grill-master. When you are eating meat try think of it more as a garnish rather than the main event. For example, on a panini retire the ham from first fiddle and make it just one of the many players in your sandwich symphony. By giving the tomatoes, cucumbers, spouts, and cheese an equally important role to the meat you are creating beautiful skinny music that will have your heart and body singing along with glee.

Exercise

Just as proper nutrition will help you lose weight, so will exercise. As an added benefit exercise will go a long way in changing not only the size but also the shape of your body. Exercise helps you stretch, tone, and tighten your muscles. It will also make you feel amazing through the release of endorphins into your bloodstream.

You should not begin any exercise routine until you have been okayed by your doctor. For most women this is six to eight weeks after delivery. Once you have been given the green light, jump in with these creative new mommy workout tips.

Do something every (week) day - Make it your mission to move your body at least once every day from Monday - Friday. Think of it a bit like your job. You can take the weekend off but you have to work it during the week. You don't have to be sweating at baby boot camp every morning, but make an effort to do something that gets your blood pumping for at least 20 minutes. A quick stroller walk around the block will do the trick. As a bonus you and baby will get some fresh air and new scenery to explore together.

Wear your baby - Pop your little cupcake into a Bjorn, Beco, or sling and go about your daily activities. Pick up the house, vacuum, or chat on the phone. Do whatever you normally would, just do it with your baby in the carrier. The weight of the baby adds resistance to help you burn extra calories, build muscle strength, and tone your body. All as you simply go about your daily activities. Wearing your baby is also great for bonding. Baby will love being snuggled up nice and close to his mama. When wearing your baby, try to keep your shoulders back and down. Avoid slumping forward as this can lead to poor posture and back stiffness.

If you haven't had luck with baby carriers, don't be afraid to go to a baby boutique and ask for a sales associate to show you how to use it properly. I struggled for weeks to figure out how to put my daughter in all the positions that were outlined in the instructional diagram. No amount of *You Tube* could help me figure it out. It wasn't until my Mommy and Me teacher showed me how to properly use the carrier in various positions that my daughter warmed up to baby wearing.

Make best friends with your stroller - To score a fabulous new mommy body, your stroller is the best exercise tool you have. No matter how little you feel like working out it shouldn't be too hard to convince yourself to go for a walk. Just a walk. Tell yourself you can take it as slow and leisurely as you want. That doesn't sound so bad does it? Once you get out there and the endorphins are flowing try a quick power walk or head up a steep hill. Going up an incline is wonderful for your legs, gluts, and the *buhthigh (that cute spot where your butt hits your thigh)*. Walking at a brisk pace burns about 400 calories per hour. That means getting out an hour per day, five days a week, will shave off an additional 2-4 pounds per month. Keep that up for three months and that is an extra 10 pounds! Stroller walking is extra wonderful because it is something that you and your little one can do together. Your babe will probably even catch some extra zzzz's while you are toning your hot mommy bod.

Baby friendly exercise programs - Finding someone to watch your baby while you work out can be tough to coordinate. Instead look for programs that incorporate baby into the fitness routine or offer child care. If you like the idea of working out with your baby, check out programs like *Stroller Strides* or *Stroller Fit*. These classes turn your stroller into a portable fitness device (think stability bar for lunges) and connect you with other fitness minded mamas in your area. For a more gentle work out try baby yoga. Classes incorporate baby into traditional yoga poses to help build strength and flexibility. Many even offer a little bonus yoga or massage as a special treat for baby. If there are no studios offering baby yoga in your area order a DVD from *Amazon.com* and try it out at home. If you prefer solo work out sessions, check out gyms that offer complimentary childcare. Many major chains like *Lifetime* and *LA Fitness* have this as a benefit of membership.

Snack-er-cize - It can be tricky to find a dedicated chunk of time to set aside for exercise, especially when your baby is still very young. Instead grab quick 'snacks' of exercise all day long. Spend two minutes working your biceps by lifting baby up and down over your chest. Sneak in three sets of ten lunges and squats while you are on the phone or washing bottles. Do push-ups over your baby while he is lying on his play mat. For extra motivation, offer baby a kiss every time you complete a rep. You can also develop associations that remind you to snack-er-cize. For example every time you are at a red light flex and tighten your stomach until the light turns green. Every little bit counts!

Put it on your calendar - If you find a program or class you enjoy make a point to sign up for it in advance. Once it is on your calendar it will be harder to blow off. Consider pre-paying for the class to give you an extra incentive to show up. Even if it is just an appointment with yourself to go for a power walk, schedule the time in your calendar. To get more serious, strap yourself with a penalty, like having to return a recently bought item of clothing, if you miss the appointment. When you know you need to be somewhere at a specific time you can work your day around it, planning naps and feedings such that they will not coincide with the appointment. Scheduling helps minimize excuses and possible interruptions so that you can get your body moving.

Let go of the guilt - If you are the type of mommy that prefers to work out sans baby, it can be difficult to prioritize this time just for you. You may feel guilt leaving your baby to do something so 'selfish.' You might even feel that your husband, or whoever you leave the baby with while you exercise, is judging you for taking this time away. Let go of this. Remember that taking care of yourself will give you more energy and desire to take care of those around you. Denying yourself simple pleasures like exercise is a great way to build resentment towards your new lifestyle and can cause tension within your family. Keep yourself in positive spirits and tip-top shape by taking some time just for you.

A friend shared with me her philosophy that mommy guilt is the most wasted emotion in the world. I think she's right. As moms we constantly evaluate if we are doing the right thing and worry that we've made the wrong choices. This comes with the territory. No matter what we do or which choices we make we will probably always feel that we could have done things differently or better. Try to let go of the guilt and focus on the positive instead.

Carefully focus on your abs - Up to two out of three women experience some rectus diastasis (abdominal separation) after child birth. It often shows up as a faint line down the middle of your stomach. To check if you have separation lie flat on your back, place your finger tips on your belly button and curl up. If you can feel a gap that is more than a finger and a half wide you may have some experienced separation. The good news is that this can be healed within about six months. Performing the right abdominal exercises consistently, ideally a few minutes every day, will help reverse the separation. Exercises that are good for healing rectus diastasis are those that engage the core without applying additional stress on the muscles. Good exercises include planks, pelvic floor lifts, and crunches on a stability ball. Avoid anything that puts stress on the abs or pulls them apart such as unsupported sit ups, burpies, or yoga poses like updog and cow.

Set a goal - If you are the type that thrives on having a goal to work towards, consider signing up for an upcoming athletic event like a 10K run, rollerblading marathon, or bike race. After having a baby, you are now aware your body is amazing and capable of ANYTHING. Take on that mindset and know that even a marathon is nothing compared to birthing your baby. Purchase an appropriate stroller or bike trailer to train for the event and get going! To use most of this equipment your baby needs to have full head control, which usually happens around 6-10 months. So this type of event is best for maintaining your hot body, not losing the initial weight.

Get a buddy - Add a little peer pressure to your workouts by making a fitness appointment with a friend. If you know it is hard for you to self-motivate, having a work out buddy is a great way to get yourself not only into your workout clothes but actually out the door. Make sure to choose a friend that is also highly motivated to work out, because peer pressure can work both ways. It is way easier to bail on a workout if both of you don't want to go. My favorite running partner and I once made it around the block only to end up at an Italian restaurant drinking martinis and eating pasta. If this sounds more like you and your friends consider joining a group. I got much better results after joining a running club with a dozen other motivated joggers and an instructor to keep us in check. Websites like **www.seemommyrun.com** and companies like the *Running Room / Walking Room* have groups across the country. Joining a club makes it much less likely you will end up like me, full and drunk in your running shorts after a 'workout'.

Create a mini-home gym - If you find it tough to get to the gym, don't live close to one, or just plain don't like them, bring the gym to you. Pick a place in your home where you feel comfortable and have enough space to work out. With a small set of hand weights, a resistance band, and a mat you have everything you need to get a great workout. If you don't want to purchase equipment, you can swap soup cans for the hand weights and soft carpet for the mat. If you want guidance in your workout, pick up an instructional DVD. There are plenty of exercise DVD options from aerobics to yoga to pole dancing. Select the one that is most exciting to you and get moving!

Dance with your baby - Not only is dancing a great workout but it is also a great opportunity to bond with your baby. Your little one will love the movement and being snuggled up close to mom. Aim to keep your boogie going through four songs, or more if you can. Use baby's gurgles and giggles as your motivation to keep going.

Taking care of your body is perhaps the best thing you can do for yourself after having a baby. Not only will you look better, you will feel better too. A healthy lifestyle will help you to cope with sleep deprivation and give you the energy you need to keep up with your little one. And did I mention you will look hot? There is absolutely no better style accessory than a rockin' body. Keep your eyes on the prize and your hands off the cookies!

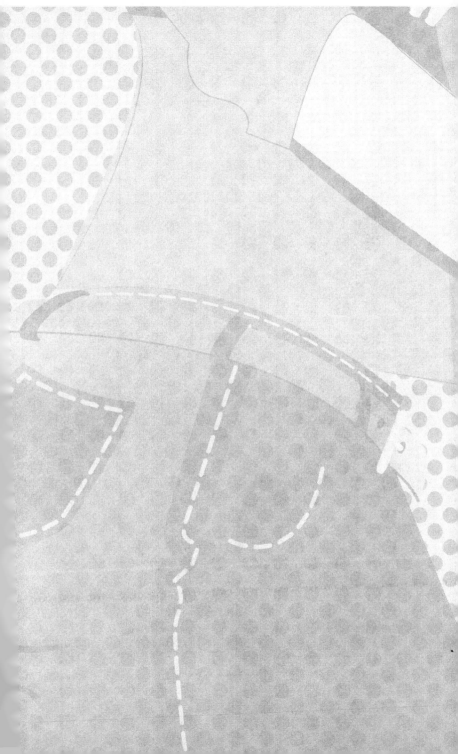

CHAPTER 5

Baby Gear

WHEN YOU FIND out you are pregnant, not only are you overjoyed that in nine short months you will be welcoming the new love of your life to the world, you also get to go SHOPPING! There is no better excuse for a splurge than the arrival of a new baby. She has to be welcomed in style, right? But before you go and blow your shoe savings on a bunch of new baby gear, get clear on which things you really need, and what you can go without. A little bit of pre-planning may help save your pennies, and your sanity.

When I was pregnant, one of the things I was looking most forward to was registering. When the big day finally came, I was so excited to get to baby store and gush over all things sugar and spice. Entering the first hundred-thousand-square-foot baby mega store was exhilarating! My eyes scanned the space pausing on teeny tiny outfits, trendy patterned strollers, and soft sumptuous blankets. Then we started down the aisles. My excitement evaporated. I was absolutely overwhelmed. Who knew there were twenty types of pacifiers? How complicated must nursing be if an entire section of the store was dedicated to breast-pumping equipment? Three hours passed by in an absolute blur. My husband and I drove home in silence, desperately trying to re-cooperate and calm our rising anxiety.

I wish I could say that the baby gear buying experience got easier after she arrived. Unfortunately, I continued to struggle with what to buy as she entered each new stage and saw new, innovative products. I wanted to keep her happy and entertained, but I also didn't want to blow our retirement savings cluttering up our home with giraffe-themed baby paraphernalia. Read on for some stylish baby gear recommendations that will help you sort through what you need and what you don't.

Strollers

In a perfect world you would have only one, fabulous stroller. Practically however, you will probably have two or three. One main character and one or two supporting cast members.

The main character (your everyday stroller) - Your primary stroller is the one you should spend the most time selecting and will likely be the most expensive. Strollers are kind of like cars. In their essence, they are simply designed to get you from A to B. However, you will enjoy the ride a lot more if they come with a few extra bells and whistles. For those with a long commute, the additional features on higher-end, luxury models are worth their cost. For those that don't, it can be wiser to choose a more basic model.

If you are taking a short maternity leave, live in a very cold climate, or simply don't find the idea of long, frequent walks very appealing, don't waste your money on a fancy celebrity stroller just to have it sit in your garage. Instead, check out *Chicco, Baby Trend,* and *Graco,* available at major retailers like *Babies R Us, Target,* and *Wal-Mart*. They all make good, basic strollers that should more than suit your everyday needs.

If you have been looking more forward to picking out a stroller than you did your last pair of *Citizens* (and you plan on using it - a lot!), then check out some more premium options at your local baby boutique or online. Most high-end strollers are European made, or at least European-inspired. *Peg Perego, Orbit, Mutsy, iCandy, Stokke,* and of course the *Bugaboo* are popular luxury European stroller systems. If you prefer to buy something made on this side of the ocean, *Teutonia* and *Uppa Baby* are comparable brands from the USA. While these strollers cost two to five times a basic *Graco* they come with oodles of features and, of course, huge style points.

The main thing that differentiates these strollers from the rest of the pack is that most are modular. A modular stroller is essentially a frame that can accommodate many different components. Meaning you could fit a bassinet, infant car seat, or baby seat on the same frame! Often the seats can be snapped in so that they face either forwards or backwards. You can also purchase accessories like shopping bags and cup holders to accommodate a shopping or *Starbucks* obsession. In addition to looking great, these strollers also roll like a dream. Some even have built-in shock absorbers to ensure a comfy, smooth ride for baby and a more effortless pushing experience for you. If you are having a hard time justifying the expense of a fancy stroller and need a little push, consider this: premium strollers tend to hold their value over time. If you keep your chariot in good condition you can often resell it for 40-70% of the original cost, making the actual cash outlay close to what you would have paid for a standard stroller.

No matter which brand you choose, select a model that can accommodate your infant car seat. Being able to snap your car seat into the stroller, without taking your baby out of the seat, is a handy feature that will save you from waking (read: aggravating) him when you transition from car to stroller or vice versa. Every mommy knows there is nothing that makes you feel less fab than a shrieking baby.

Supporting cast member #1 (your travel stroller) ~ If travel is a part of your life, you should consider purchasing a stroller for the road, especially if you bought a more expensive everyday stroller. Leaving a $700+ piece of equipment in the care of the airlines is not something I would be exactly excited about doing. Everyday strollers can also be awkward and heavy to carry. They can also take up a lot of room in your trunk. Having a lightweight, inexpensive travel stroller is a great way to lighten your travel load and keep from looking like one of those mommies who brought the contents of their entire house with them on the road. Travelling light = chic.

If you don't travel often, a gently used umbrella stroller from a second hand shop is a nice, inexpensive option. Look for one with a five point harness, especially if your baby is still small. If you plan on doing a substantial amount of travel, you may want to purchase a new travel stroller. There is no need to spend a fortune even if you buy new. The most important part of the stroller is that it is lightweight and easy to carry. Look for one that has a shoulder strap, weighs less than twelve pounds, and is not more than $150. Coming in at less than ten pounds, the *Maclaren Volo* is a popular choice, as is the *Chicco C6*, and the *Graco IPO*.

If your baby is still very young, and you are more comfortable snapping her infant car seat into a stroller system, consider buying a Snap n' Go frame for travel. *Baby Trend* and *Graco* both make frames with ample carrying baskets that are compatible with most car seat brands. As a bonus, the frame is basic silver and black so it coordinates with any car seat.

Supporting cast member #2 (your athletic stroller) - Before you rush out and buy a jogging stroller ask yourself an important question. Do I jog? Not, am I going to start jogging? *Do – I – jog?* Did I jog before the baby? I hate to burst your bubble but no matter how well intentioned you are to get back in shape by running, if you weren't a runner before you probably aren't going to become one just after having a baby. If I haven't convinced you to save your money, at least promise that you will wait four months until buying one. Babies shouldn't be put in a jogger until they have full head control (usually around 6-10 months) so you can't use it in the first few months anyways. If you end up using your spare time those first few months going for runs while your hubby watches the little one, good for you. You have earned your new jogging stroller! If not, save the cash and buy a cute pair of shades instead.

I'll admit, I bought a jogging stroller. I don't jog. I really wanted to start jogging. But I don't jog. I used the stroller three times in the first year I owned it. Sad. Luckily, I purchased it second hand from a friend so I was only out $20. I was excited when I got it because it was basically new. My friend had three kids and had only used it a few times. I should have seen the lesson here. Now I now have an extra piece of baby gear that I don't want or need cluttering up my garage. Heed the advice, only buy a jogger if you are a jogger!

If you do buy an athletic stroller, test drive the widely popular *BOB Revolution* or less expensive *Jeep Overland.* If you are serious about fitness and cross training, you probably want the *BOB Ironman.* While the bright yellow color is somewhat polarizing, the technical makeup of this stroller is ideal for the serious athlete and is designed to handle rough terrain and long excursions.

If you aren't necessarily an athlete but are looking for a stroller that will handle long rides on bumpy ground, you might consider a three wheel athletic stroller from a brand like *phil and teds.* Both their *Classic* and *Explorer* buggies are built to handle rougher rides. If more babies are in your plans, not only do those models look great, they also convert to accommodate two children.

Please only buy a three wheel athletic stroller if you plan to use it outside or for athletics. Don't purchase a stroller like this as your everyday stroller, unless of course your everyday activities include hiking in the mountains or traversing bumpy roads. There is nothing worse than watching a fellow mommy try to maneuver a large three wheel, all-terrain stroller while shopping at the mall or wandering through a museum. It looks as awkward as a woman pushing her baby down the sidewalk in 5-inch Manolos. Style victim! No matter how cool something looks, if it's not practical for your life, don't buy it!

If you choose to buy an athletic stroller, you might have luck at a consignment shop, on *Craigslist,* or *eBay*. Many mommies buy an all-terrain stroller expecting they will use it to run but never get around to it. Second hand can be a great way to score a great stroller at a steal of a price.

No matter which stroller(s) you purchase, scout out those with subtle patterns. While the fuchsia, indigo, mint, and yellow flower pattern may look super cute in the store, once you add to it a baby dressed in pink and brown polka dots holding a bright blue and orange doll wrapped in a pale yellow blanket, it can start to look a bit much. Keeping the stroller patterns and colors to a minimum will make the stroller look more stylish when there is actually a baby in it (which is 99% of the time). Also, if you plan to use the stroller for more than one baby, pick one in a neutral color like grey, khaki, black, or brown to make sure it can accommodate either gender. You can turn up the little girl or little guy factor with colorful throw blankets, toys, and accessories.

Finally, look for something that is easy to fold and fits in the trunk of your car. It sounds obvious, but you wouldn't be the first mommy to buy a stroller and have to cart it around folded in your backseat. Awkward never equals fabulous.

Car Seats

While you can technically buy a convertible car seat that can be used from birth through childhood, don't. Even the biggest of newborns still look far too fragile to be placed in one of those large car seats. I suggest buying an infant seat for the first 6-12 months, then a convertible seat for the remaining years.

I wish I could provide a long list of style savvy car seat options, but the reality is that car seats really just aren't very stylish. I remember cringing when I'd get into co-workers cars that had the standard beige or grey cloth seat taking up fifty percent of their backseat. That will never be me I would think. I'll find a trendy looking seat that looks like a fabulous car accessory instead of a cloth and plastic monstrosity. I didn't. When it comes to choosing a car seat there are a few style points to consider, but for the most part these seats are ugly. Sigh.

Infant seat - Infant seats are not only cozy, they are also extremely practical. They snap into strollers, fit in shopping carts, and can be carried over the arm for a quick dash into *Starbucks* for a decaf skinny vanilla Frappuccino. Your baby will probably outgrow the infant bucket in length long before he gets too heavy for it. For this reason don't be too concerned if the seat holds up to 22lbs or 35lbs. It is unlikely you would ever use it for a child this heavy anyways. Opt for a lighter seat, likely one that accommodates up to 22lbs, to ease the strain on your back from hoisting it in and out of the car.

The ideal car seat should be i) safe (duh) ii) compatible with your chosen stroller iii) fit in your car. Since all car seats sold in the USA are safety-tested you should feel confident selecting most any brand. *Peg Pergo* is the Volvo of car seats, however it is heavier than most. The *Maxi Cosi* is a great looking, imported seat from Europe and is also well-rated, but be warned that it is not compatible with many American strollers. *Graco, Safety 1st,* and *Chicco* are among the most popular seats in the US. They are all safe and highly compatible with most strollers. It is likely you will find one within those brands that meets your needs. Don't be afraid to ask the salesperson to help you set it up in your car to make sure it fits. Car seats can be bulky and, especially if you have a small or mid-sized car, may be a tight squeeze. This is another reason to buy a lighter, smaller car seat.

For the same reasons as with strollers, look for car seats with subtle patterns and gender-neutral colors. Many infant car seats can be bought with a stroller as a set. This is a nice option to ensure everything matches. If you don't purchase yours as a system, pay extra attention to patterns so your pieces don't clash!

Convertible seat - As your baby gets heavier, the infant car seat will feel less and less fabulous. Around 15-20 lbs., most moms let go of their infant buckets and purchase a second car seat. Look for a seat that can face both front and rear and, ideally, can be converted into booster once your little one outgrows needing a car seat. This way it will be the last car seat you ever need to buy.

Unlike your infant seat, look for one that does not have a base, especially if you travel a lot. Having to travel with a car seat base adds unnecessary bulk to your packing. A base also adds cost to the unit, especially if you buy one for each vehicle. Wouldn't you prefer to spend those dollars on an amazing first birthday outfit and matching party hat? If your car(s) has a latch system (and most made in the last fifteen years do) it takes only a moment to secure the car seat. It should be easy to switch the seat between cars if needed, even without a base. *Evenflo, Britax,* and *Graco* all make a selection of seats that should meet your needs. This seat will remain in your car for the next four years, or until your baby reaches 40lbs. Yes, four years. So, buy a seat that you don't mind looking at and ideally coordinates with your car interior.

Nursery Furniture

The only truly essential item in your baby nursery is somewhere for your baby to sleep. A crib, cradle, bassinet, or co-sleeper will do the trick. In addition, a rocking chair or glider makes new mommy life much easier by allowing you to feed baby in the middle of the night without leaving the nursery. Beyond those two things, consider EVERYTHING optional. Do you really need a wipe warmer and a mobile over your changing table? Most mommies end up changing diapers on the floor, making the changing table an unnecessary purchase. If there is room in the closet for your little one's teeny tiny outfits, a dedicated baby dresser or wardrobe may be totally unnecessary for you. Aside from the crib, the pieces you select depend entirely on your taste, budget, and available space.

Crib frame - Obviously you need a crib. What you don't need is a crib that costs thousands of dollars. Look for something that is sturdy, visually appealing, and less than $500. Unless you have really specific tastes you should be able to find something beautiful without breaking the bank. If you want your nursery to have a modern or contemporary feel, search out a crib with clean, straight lines in espresso or white. If you are more traditional, look for a cherry or mahogany finish on a sleigh style crib.

Mattress - The mattress also need not be expensive. As long as it is firm and the right size for the crib, it will work. It is easy to get upsold to a fabulous mattress in organic cotton, until you realize that all that amazing organic cotton gets covered with sheets. It's only a mattress. Your little one's ten pound self won't make a much different impact on a mattress that costs $50 or $500. Save your money to invest in something more style-worthy.

Bedding - When selecting crib bedding pick style over quality. You will be changing sheets often and occasionally even throwing them away. So don't get carried away selecting posh sheets. Since your baby is usually fully covered in pajamas or a swaddling blanket, her precious skin won't even touch the sheets. Don't worry too much about the thread count.

Mobiles - Some babies love mobiles. Others could care less. If you find an adorable mobile that goes with your décor, snatch it up. If not, don't stress about getting this baby 'essential.'

Newborn-crib - Some parents do not want to put their little one into a big crib right after birth. Instead, you can opt for a bassinet, pack & play, or cradle. If you buy something for this purpose, just remember that within a couple months you will likely transition to the crib. The piece you are purchasing will only be used for a matter of weeks. So try not to buy something that has no purpose after those few uses. While a teeny wooden rocking cradle is adorable, it will just take up space in your basement once your baby is a few months old. You'll be wishing you had the money back to buy frilly baby socks and tiny swimming suits. A more practical choice is a pack & play that will be useful long after your baby is transitioned to his crib. Another option is to purchase a bassinet that is compatible with your stroller. Many modular stroller brands, like *Uppa Baby* and *Bugaboo*, have bassinets designed to clip into the stroller frames. Using your bassinet both as a mini crib and as a stroller helps to justify the investment. As an additional bonus, the bassinet can be placed directly in the crib so that your little one will get used to his big crib, while still snuggled up in his little bassinet.

Rocking chair/glider - No matter how chic the white armless curved wooden rocker looks in your *CB2* catalogue, the backache you will get on day eight of rocking and feeding your little one will not be worth it. Having a comfortable chair to feed, rock, and cuddle your baby in is worth it's weight in diamonds. This is one piece where it is worth sacrificing a little bit of style for comfort. You can always dress up the chair with a chic throw and pillows to add style points while you aren't using it. To get the best bang for your investment, select a chair that might get a second life after you are done using it in the nursery. By choosing a more sophisticated fabric, your chair may find new life as a reading spot in your bedroom or lounge chair in your husband's man cave.

I really wanted a chic white leather (non-reclining) arm chair with a fab sparkly silver accent pillow for our nursery. Even though I knew the fabric would stain and the pillow was scratchy, it looked so great with our crib and paint. Thank goodness my husband talked me out of that one. I don't often admit when he is right, but this was one of those times. Instead, we settled on an oversized dark paisley glider that coordinated with our living room décor and reclined all the way flat. I am so grateful for that comfortable chair in the middle of the night. I cringe to think how cold and silly white leather would feel at 3am. I was able to dress up the chair with a great silver throw to coordinate with the nursery and despite all the spit up the chair shows no evidence after a quick wipe. I love that we will be able to repurpose it in our living room once our daughter grows out of midnight snuggles (which secretly I hope is no time soon).

Baby 'Furniture'

There are four baby 'furniture' essentials: a swing, a bouncy chair, a play mat, and a pack & play. That's it. Four essentials. Just four! Beyond these four basic items be cautious of what you bring into your home. While it is tempting to give your sweetie pie the chance to experience everything, you may end up just creating clutter with a bunch of apparatus that your baby doesn't use very often. If a girlfriend has something you are interested in, like a jumper, *Exersaucer*, or *Bumbo*, ask to borrow it first to make sure your little one likes it. Babies are fickle and what they like one day they may not love next week. Before you spend your money and haul another box home from the baby store, make sure your little one will use what you are buying.

Your four essentials will likely live in your living room, so you should select gear you don't mind looking at. You will be looking at it a lot. These items can be stored away when you have company, but because you will use them pretty much every day they will start to feel as permanent to you as your TV, sofa, and dining table. For this reason, I suggest purchasing your four gear essentials as a matching set. Choose a color and pattern that is easy on your eyes. If your home is nicely appointed with soft gold, butter, and auburn tones a matched set of cream and brown gear would be a nice option. If you have a funky modern pad decked out in bright white, blue, and crisp green you might be able to get away with a deep blue under-water themed set. While your gear will never exactly match your décor (nor should it!), you can find ways to make it complementary. The goal is for it not to stick out the way your husband would attempting goddess pose in prenatal yoga.

Swing - If there was only one piece of essential baby gear this would be it. While you do hear of the occasional baby that hates the swing, in general this plastic miracle is a bonafide mommy savior. Most babies love the gentle rocking motion that lulls them to sleep, often for much longer than they will stay snoozing in a crib. Many swings also have interesting mobiles or mirrors for the baby to look at which can provide loads of entertainment even when they are awake. To maximize the likelihood that your baby will fall in love with the swing look for one that can swing both side to side and front to back, like the *Fisher-Price My Little Lamb* or *Starlight Papasan*. As a bonus, both of these swings are nicely neutral to help blend with most decors.

Bouncy chair - The bouncer is great for when you want to put your little one down but don't want to put him on the floor. The cuddly chair will comfort your baby almost as snugly as an extra pair of arms. I like to keep my bouncer in the bathroom and use it when I grab a shower, blow dry my hair, or put on my make-up. If you purchased a modular stroller, you might be able to purchase an attachment to convert the seat into a bouncy chair, instead of buying a separate bouncer. *Mutsy,* for example, sells a base for around $20 that their *4 Rider* stroller seat clips into. Voilà, bouncy chair! This not only saves you some cash, it keeps you from adding one more plastic baby contraption to your home décor.

Play mat - For the first six months of your baby's life (or until she becomes mobile) the play mat will be like your baby's best friend. Don't be scared to get the brightest, gaudiest one at the store. It can easily be stashed under a coffee table or couch when it is not in use. Likely, the brighter and louder the mat, the more fun your baby will have playing with it (and the longer you will have to catch up with your *US Weekly*).

Pack & play - For the next six months of your baby's life (or after she becomes mobile) the pack and play will be like *your* best friend. Keep it stocked with a few favorite play things and get in the habit of putting your baby in it once per day. Getting your sweetie used to hanging out in her playpen will not only help her learn independent play skills, it will also free your hands up to fix a healthy dinner or flat iron your hair. The pack and play will be stationary most of the time, so place it as carefully as you would furniture and choose an aesthetic that you like. If you plan on using the pack and play as a crib for travel, also look for one that is lightweight and easy to carry like the *Cosco Funsport*.

Toys

Avoid cluttering up your fabulous home with bright loud toys by using your creativity and finding ways to entertain baby with things you already own. You will be surprised by what you have around your house that babies will find fun to play with.

Your closet - Show her the many textures in your closet. Your baby will love touching your silky scarfs, soft pajamas, and fuzzy sweaters.

The kitchen - When he gets a little bit older pots, pans, and brightly hued Tupperware can double as a drum set or simple play toys.

The bookshelf - In addition to baby books you can catch up on news and fashion trends by reading newspapers, magazines, or catalogs to her. She loves the sound of your voice and the pictures. It won't matter to her what type of book you are reading.

The junk drawer - Try making your own flash cards by taking plain white index cards and drawing simple shapes on them with a thick black marker. Or try scattering a few playing cards on the floor and watch your darling push them around and pick them up. If you really want to spoil your pumpkin, treat him to an old remote (no batteries) or oversized calculator.

The fridge - Many babies love plastic bottles. Give him a water bottle and let him experience what it feels like empty, partially full, and totally full. He will love touching it, shaking it, and rolling it around.

Toilet paper - Ok so maybe this one isn't exactly a toy and admitting I let my little girl play with this probably won't help my application for mother of the year. However, every once and a while when I'm desperate for a hot shower and a deep exfoliation, I let my daughter unroll the paper on the holder while I watch her through the glass shower door. Even though it wastes the paper, and probably doesn't teach a good habit, every once in a while I just get desperate. As a bonus, the toilet paper core makes a fun toy to roll on the floor or sing into.

Layette (Clothing) & Accessories

Arguably, the most fun part of baby shopping is picking out those oh-too-cute-for-words mini outfits in every color, shape, pattern, and size. Before you go too crazy loading up your cart with clothing, take a few moments to picture your baby wearing it. Do you see a sporty baby clad in mini sweats and teeny jogging pants? Frilly pink ballerina skirts and sparkly barrettes? Eclectic logo T's, distressed jeans and booties? Bloomers and bonnets? The way you dress is a reflection of your personal style and, more than likely, you will be drawn to a certain style for your baby as well. You may not know what this is exactly until you meet your little one. Is she sweet and calm, feisty and stubborn, or dreamy and mellow? As tough as it is, try to hold off on purchasing the majority of the clothing until you have met your baby and know what suits her.

<u>*Everyday outfits*</u> - Because babies grow so quickly there is (sigh) the possibility that he will outgrow that adorable little urban cowboy outfit you

splurged on before he ever gets a chance to wear it. The good news is that this happens to other mommies too. Meaning, second hand stores are packed with über-cute baby outfits, often in pristine condition. For the best selection, prioritize the second hand stores in the nicest neighborhoods. In general, the nicer the area, the more likely you are to score high quality items (often brand new) at a fraction of the retail price.

Beyond preferences, there are also a few practical considerations when selecting baby wear. First, pick pieces that are easy to put on. Generally, the more stretch in the fabric the better. Fabric with give is easier to get on and off baby without too much fuss. Second, zippers are much easier than snaps. Look for zippers, especially on pajamas. Finally, outfits with attached bibs not only look cute but can save you loads of laundry by catching spit up before it cakes onto the outfit.

Remember that your baby will often be wrapped up in blankets, sitting in the car seat/stroller, or carting around a toy. All these things have their own colors and patterns. Having a few simple, solid color outfits will help baby to coordinate with the sea of baby patterns that surround her. Simple outfits are also great because they can be dressed up with fun accessories like socks, hats, headbands, sunglasses, and shoes.

Accessories - The same outfit can look totally different just by changing the accessories. Today there are literally thousands of adorable baby accessories that will take your breath away. If you don't believe me spend fifteen minutes on *Esty.com*. From feather applique headbands to beaded barrettes to newsboy caps and ruffled ballet socks; there is something for everyone. Baby accessories can be the cutest part of the outfit. Set them off by dressing your baby in more plain outfits when you add them.

Special outfits - Of course every baby needs a few special outfits that just scream adorable, even if they aren't super practical or clash with everything. Select what you are drawn to and get out that camera. Dressing baby is primarily for your enjoyment, so go ahead and splurge on a few fun pieces that you can't wait to see your little one in. I always enjoyed dressing my daughter up for different holidays. A few extra dollars for a baby Halloween costume or mini Santa suit is nothing to exchange for all the joyful memories and once in a lifetime pictures.

Feeding Gear

When you start feeding your baby solid foods (around 4-6 months), the one gear essential you will want to purchase is a high chair. Beyond a high chair, there a few additional items that will make mealtimes easier and more fun.

High chair ~ To keep with your home décor, especially if you have an open concept kitchen, select a high chair that coordinates with your pack & play, bouncy chair, and swing set. If not, select something that compliments your kitchen/dining décor.

If you are square foot-challenged, check out a space saving model that attaches to an existing chair like the *Fisher Price Space Saver.* A fabric attachment like the *My Little Seat* or *Baby Go* by *Evenflo* is another great option that reduces floor clutter and also doubles as a travel chair. The *Chicco travel chair* is also great for small spaces, attaching to the table if you don't have an extra chair. Just make sure your table is sturdy enough to support the extra weight.

If you have more space and are willing to make a bit more of an investment, look for a convertible model that can stay with your little one right through childhood. Convertible highchairs can be changed into a booster seat or special spot to sit for later in your child's life. The *Combi Hero* and *Stokke Tripp Trapp* are two popular models to check out.

If your little one squirms when he eats, look for a model that has some padding to save his sweet noggin from unnecessary bumps and bangs.

Baby dishes - Even baby plastic wear is cute! Your baby will eventually eat three meals a day. Purchasing a matching set of three bowls, plates, cups, and cutlery will ensure you always have what you need for mealtime. Look for bowls with suction bottoms, like the *Tommee Tippee Munchkin Stayput Suction Bowls*, to help minimize spills and keep your kitchen sparkly clean.

Bibs - Look for larger bibs to provide maximum coverage to keep your little one's outfits as clean as possible. Plastic bibs are nice as they can be wiped down or rinsed off without adding to your laundry pile. Less work AND better for the environment? Sounds like winning idea to me.

Bath Gear

Baby tub - I believe that it is just as easy to bathe your baby in the sink as in a baby tub. Before you know it your baby will outgrow the baby tub and you will have yet another bright plastic addition to add to your basement stockpile. So, before you buy a baby tub, think twice. If you are uncomfortable with the sink, you can get into the regular tub with your baby for her bath. Fill the tub with just a few inches of water and sit her on your lap. This is something that you, dad, or both of you can do together to bond with your baby.

As you baby gets older and bathes in the regular tub, don't rush to load up on bath toys. If he is happy splashing up a storm, you likely don't need a bunch of toys. However, if your little one gets bored or aggravated, a few distractions are probably a good idea. Try waterproof books or floating toys to help make bath time more fun. There are such a variety to choose from, you can likely even find a few pieces that complement your bathroom décor.

Towels and washcloths - How cute are those little hooded towels and mini patterned washcloths? Absolutely adorable. How useful are they? About the same as a regular towel and a standard washcloth. Now, I am not one to stand between a mommy and a few baby bath splurges because I agree these items are too cute for words. However, before you go purchase a dozen cloths and a half dozen hooded towels just realize that these things really are not necessary. Especially if they just sit folded up in a drawer or closet somewhere. I recommend buying as many towels and cloths as you can display. If you have a sweet baby towel hook in your bathroom, by all means buy a sweet hooded towel to display on it. Likewise, if you have a basket of baby cloths rolled up beside your tub, fill up that basket! Just don't go crazy purchasing things that you get few opportunities to use, or at least display. You can use your regular towels just as easily provided they are new(ish) and not washed in harsh detergents.

Baby Carriers

I am a huge fan of baby wearing. The freedom of being able to use your hands while holding your baby is, in my opinion, life changing. However, many mommies do not like baby wearing at all. Yet almost every new mom I have ever met owns at least one baby carrier. Few actually use them. If you don't like wearing your baby, don't buy a baby carrier!

Buy just one! - If you do like wearing your baby, try to limit yourself to buying only ONE. If you find a great carrier that you and your baby love, there is no reason to purchase additional carriers. I like the *Ergo Baby* and *Beco* because they have infant inserts which allow you to use the same carrier from birth through toddlerhood. Both are well designed to keep stress off your shoulders, back, and neck.

I was so desperate to free my hands in the first few months I ended up with more than one, um three, baby carriers. Every time I saw a mom with a baby happily snuggled up, I would ask about her carrier and go look for the same model to purchase. If it worked for her, it should work for me, right? Wrong. Those first few months can be so overwhelming it is tempting to shell out for anything that you think will make your life easier or keep your baby more comfortable. Try to hold back and use your rationality. If you have friends with carriers, ask if you can borrow one for a test run before making your purchase. If there is a friendly sales associate, you may even be able to take one for a spin in the store before making your final selection.

Lightweight & neutral - Whatever brand you choose look for a model that is light-weight (baby wearing is HOT) and made with a neutral fabric or simple pattern. You don't want your carrier clashing with your outfit or baby's layette!

Diapers & Wipes

Diapers - Buy good diapers. Of all the areas to skimp on baby gear, diapers are not one of them. This is also not the place to start saving the environment with altruistic ideas about cladding your little one's bottom in organic cloth. At the risk of sounding like a bad mom for not changing my precious little girl every time she pees, I will admit I LOVE how much fluid premium brands of disposable diapers, like *Pampers,* can hold. A good diaper can get you through an extra hour of shopping, let you hit the snooze button one extra time in the morning, and protect all those adorable outfits from ruin. All while keeping your little angel's bum dry and protecting her from an icky, ouchy red rash. If you skimp on diapers or use cloth, you will likely spend a lot of your life changing dirty diapers. When babies are little this can be more than a dozen per day! The less time you spend changing diapers, the more time you will have for inserting fabulousness into your life.

Wipes - It probably goes without saying but stock up on disposable wipes. I bought a two-year supply of *Pampers Sensitive* when I was pregnant and then never thought about them again. My husband is always quick to remind me that we can save the environment and some cash in many ways, but conserving wipes is not one of them. If it takes five wipes to get that poopy bum clean, by all means, use those wipes! Changing diapers is one of the less glam parts of new motherhood; make it easier by keeping your nursery well stocked with wipes.

Wipe warmer - Do yourself a favor and save the $40 on the wipe warmer. With the number of diapers you are going to be changing, locating a wipe warmer each time is going to be way more effort than it's worth. Chances are your baby won't even notice.

Your baby gear should reflect your personal style and make your life as a new mommy easier and even a bit more stylish. Try to (gently!) suppress that budding baby shop-a-holic inside of you. Instead, release your inner frugalista and make practical choices that won't bankrupt your new family, or add unnecessary clutter to your home and life. Happy Shopping!

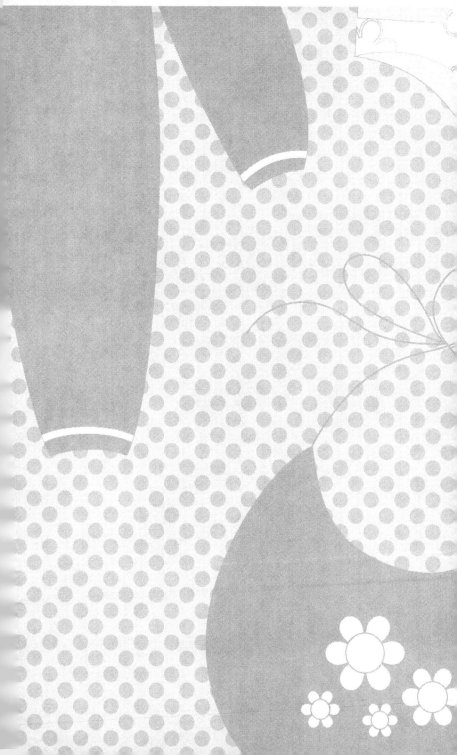

CHAPTER 6

Out and About

YOU HAVE TO GET OUT OF THE HOUSE. Read that again. You. Have. To. Get. Out. Of. The. House. Take a shower, get dressed, doll your baby up in one of the hundred adorable outfits sitting in the drawer and go do something! Part of enjoying your new life as a mommy is getting out and experiencing life with your little one. This is especially important if you are a stay-at-home mom or work part time and don't find yourself forced to leave the house frequently. An outing can be as simple as a stroller ride around the block, or as adventurous as a trip to the zoo to point out a life sized *Sophie the Giraffe*. Leaving may feel like an insurmountable task at first, but you will get better at it the more you practice. And you must practice! There is absolutely nothing fabulous about staying home all day every day. Who is going to see your new adorable new mom style from inside your pad? Get out there and show it to them!

Leaving the house can be scary for new mommies. To help tackle your fear, try these two tips. 1) At first, plan shorter outings. Ideally, be out for less than one hour. Once you get comfortable with this, try venturing out for a little bit longer. 2) Pick something you are actually excited about doing. If your outings are limited to going to the grocery store, and you hate shopping for food, you will lose your motivation to keep doing it. Lucky for you there are almost an endless number of things to do with your baby outside of your house. There is bound to be at least one activity that gets you excited to get going!

I want to...

Meet other moms - It is so common in today's society to feel isolated and alone as a new mommy. Many women move extensively for school, career, or family obligations and end up in a city without close friends or family nearby. Even those who are fortunate to have family and friends near find that sometimes after having a baby they do not connect with these people the way they once did. They yearn to find a few new mommy friends.

One great way to meet women with babies the same age as yours is through *Mommy and Me* classes. Classes usually meet once a week for six to ten weeks. Your local hospital or the Early Childhood Family Education program, **www.ecfe.com**, can help you find a class in your area. For those more religiously inclined and looking for moms who share their beliefs, check out MOPS, **www.mops.com**. If you wish to meet a little less frequently, try the international MOMS organization, **www.momsclub.org**. This group is more geared towards stay-at-home moms and typically meets monthly with a formal topic and speaker, plus informally at member's homes, parks etc.

If you just want a one-day event, try calling your local theater to see if they offer matinee movies for mommies. Many theatres offer one or two showings a month just for moms with babies. The movies are played a little quieter in a lighter room. Best of all your baby can giggle, scream, and cry all he wants and you don't have to leave the theatre.

Get some exercise - If having your baby has left you feeling lethargic and a little cushy around the middle, get excited about getting out of the house for some exercise. To keep yourself motivated and accountable, sign up for a class or make a fitness appointment with a friend. For fitness classes that incorporate your baby, check out **www.strollerfit.com** or **www.strollerstrides.com**. Call local yoga studios to see if they offer baby yoga bonding classes. If you'd rather get your sweat on baby-free, check out gyms in your area to see if they offer child care. If walking, running, or biking is more your speed, make an appointment with a friend to hit the trails. If you don't know anyone to go with, you can find a group in your area. National organizations like **www.seemommyrun.com** have over 50,000 members. There are bound to be at least a few close to you. If not, start your own chapter and bring the mommies to you! If all else fails, strap on your shoes and go for a walk somewhere that you are sure to find other mommies, like the park or the mall. Put on your bravest face and introduce yourself. Babies make for the best ice-breakers.

My first attempt at post-baby exercise was *Stroller Strides*. Admittedly, I felt pretty stupid doing lunges in the park while singing the itsy bitsy spider, but it did feel good to get out and get some fresh air. I also met a few great women who also rolled their eyes when the teacher led the group in another verse of *"If you're happy and you know it"* and ended up meeting them for power walks around the lake in lieu of class from time to time. Even though I didn't love the program, it ended up being a great way to build new friendships and some bonus (free) exercise during our meet ups.

Play with baby - Sometimes it's tricky to find things to 'do' with your baby all day at home.

You've been through the toy box (twice), cuddled, read books (nine), sang, and stared at each other for a few weeks now. You are both ready for something new. If this sounds like you and your little one, try a class specifically designed to delight, stimulate, and develop your baby.

There are a variety of class types, from infant music to little gyms to baby swimming lessons. For music, try the national organization Music Together **www.musictogether.com** to find a local class. For baby gyms, check out Gymboree **www.gymboree.com**, The Little Gym **www.thelittlegym.com**, or My Gym **www.my-gym.com**. For swimming, visit your local YMCA or YWCA. Most places will offer a free trial class so shop around and try a few options out before purchasing a package or membership.

In addition to classes, you can also check out your local library, bookstores, and toy stores for special events. Most have at least one story time hour per week plus additional special events, often around the holidays. The park is also a great option. The simple change in scenery is interesting for baby and the fresh air is good for both of you.

Learn something – If you are looking to acquire a new skill that will assist you in your new mommy life, consider taking a class or workshop. Infant massage, baby sign language, and sleep training are a few hot tickets to consider. Such courses are often offered at your local hospital, yoga studio, or community center. Workshops are a great option if you don't want to commit too much time. They are usually just a couple of hours over a one or two day period. In addition to meeting other like-minded mommies, you will also pick up some new skills that you can practice with your baby at home.

Explore my city – If you are the type that was constantly exploring your city before you had a baby, don't let mommyhood hold you back now! There are plenty of baby-friendly places to visit no matter where you live. In fact, you now have an excuse to venture outside your usual haunts and check out some new places, like the zoo! Zoos have tons of fun smells, sights, and sounds for baby. The large open space is stroller-friendly and admission is usually reasonable. Similarly, the aquarium is another great option, especially on a rainy day, as most of the exhibits are indoors. Outdoor gardens – whether they are sculpture, rose, tea, or Japanese – are fun places for baby on a nice day. Not only do you get to enjoy nature, your baby's cries won't disturb the peace the way they might in an art gallery or quaint museum. Farmer's markets also make great outings for you and your baby. Leave the stroller at home and pop your little one in a baby carrier to make it easier to weave around the stands. As a bonus, you can pick up a healthy dinner, and probably something handmade and adorable for your baby too. Finally, check out your local paper (the one you are probably currently using as a fire starter) for fun family-friendly events in your area. Local papers and community newsletters are hidden gold mines for fabulous new mommy fun.

How long do you want to be out?

Under an hour

Stroll around the neighborhood

Run an errand like dry cleaning or going to the bank

Go to *Starbucks* and write a few thank you notes (for all the great baby gifts, or anything else you are thankful for in your life)

Pick up lunch at a quick service eatery that serves fresh healthy food, like *Chipotle*

Grab groceries at a local grocer

Get your eyebrows waxed

Pick up books from the library (pre-order them online first!)

1-2 hours

Go to a friend's house for coffee

Shop for everyday essentials at *Target* or *Wal-Mart*

Take a class or workshop

Power walk with your stroller

Browse for fabulous new mommy clothes at the mall

Go to the park

Meet your husband for lunch

Volunteer visiting seniors at a retirement home. They will love meeting your little one!

2-4+ hours

Go to the zoo, aquarium, or arboretum

Drive to the outlet mall and do some shopping

Have lunch at a farmer's market

Go to a sporting event like a basketball, baseball, or football game

Combine any two shorter events into one trip

Now that you are excited about the world that exists outside your playroom let's talk about how to make it happen. There are few tricks that seasoned mommies have shared when it comes to leaving the house. Here are a few of my favorites.

Leave immediately after a feeding - Most babies are on their best behavior right after filling their tummies with a full bottle of sweet sweet breast milk or formula. Think of the pleasure you get after a nice slice of double chocolate cake and multiple that by about a thousand. This is also the time he is as far as possible away from needing another feeding. Feeding your baby on the road is by no means impossible but it will make your outing a bit easier, at least at first, if you keep this potential complication out of the equation.

I learned this lesson the hard way. I had taught my daughter to expect a feeding about every three hours. About two and a half hours after her last one I decided on a quick trip to the mall. I fled from the shoe racks with my screaming bundle of angry and dashed across the cold parking lot to the safety of my car. There no one could hear my baby cry, or watch me struggle to feed her. I turned on the radio and tried to discretely breastfeed in the parking lot. When she finally finished, I tried to turn on the engine to reveal a dead battery. Ooops. There I was, stranded in the parking lot in the middle of the cold Minnesota winter. Thank you again to the kind staff at the neighboring *Westin* that generously jumped my car so that I could get home.

Keep an emergency baby kit in your car - This kit should contain an extra outfit, pacifier, diapers/wipes, gauzy blanket that could double as a nursing shield if needed, burp cloth, toy that you know your baby loves (in absence of this a cell phone or anything with buttons in your purse will do the trick), a hat, and socks. You don't need to carry an overstuffed bag everywhere you go, but having a few essentials in the trunk of your car in case of emergency adds an extra element of comfort to any mom on the go.

Use a calendar - I prefer an online calendar like *Microsoft Outlook*. Use it to schedule the events you have going on each day. Add regular baby classes, play dates, and even appointments with yourself like going for a power walk. The more you schedule, the more you will feel accountable to show up for your planned events. Translation: you will do more things! You will also visually see how you are spending your days, which can help you feel more accomplished at the end of each week. Spend 5 minutes each evening reviewing and getting excited for what you have planned for the next day.

Keeping a calendar of my planned activities was one of the most effective tools I found to keep me motivated and satisfied with how I was spending my time day-to-day during my maternity leave. Especially when you are staying at home, days can start to blur together and it can feel that you aren't accomplishing much. No one except a mom understands just how much it takes to simply keep the baby alive and happy from the time he gets up to when he goes to bed! By having a record of what I had done during the week, and what I had to look forward to, I felt more productive and accomplished.

Create reoccurring appointments - Try to have at least a few events that happen regularly. This will help give your days, weeks, and months a cadence and you'll have activities to look forward to. Classes are great for this. Knowing that you go to *Mommy and Me* every Monday morning, baby yoga each Wednesday afternoon, and music class every Thursday evening will provide structure to your weeks and break up the feeling that Monday is like Tuesday is like Friday. Look for events beyond classes that can become regular appointments too. For example, if your husband can get out of work for lunch, plan to meet him the first Tuesday of every month at noon. (He will also appreciate your advance planning.)

Treat it like a job - While taking care of your little one is probably the most rewarding experience of your life to date, it is still a lot of work. It is a job like any other.

Treat getting out of the house as one of the requirements of your career as a mommy. Set a goal to get out of the house every day, Monday through Friday. Treat getting dressed and ready as another one of your job requirements. It is much easier to slump around the house all day if you haven't showered and are still in your pjs. Simply putting yourself together each morning will make you feel more motivated and excited to get out and about.

Savor your time at home - You won't leave the house every single day. There is nothing wrong with taking a few days off and bunking in. On the days you don't go out, indulge yourself. Spend all day in comfy loungewear, snuggle and play with your baby, or take an extra-long shower or hot bath while your sweetie naps. Enjoying your days 'off' (not leaving the house) will help to re-energize you and keep you looking forward to the outings you have coming up.

Take a deep breath - Yes, you will get caught, at least once and probably at the most inopportune time, with an inconsolable screaming baby. Keep in mind the baby sounds the loudest to you and not everyone around you. Onlookers are not judging you and whispering that you are a terrible mother. Actually, probably the opposite is happening. Those that do notice your fussing baby are probably parents themselves. As parents, they are relating to you with a quiet smile and a memory of when their baby did something similar. Catch their eyes, my bet is they are friendly and full of admiration for you and the great job you are doing as a mommy. So, the next time your baby melts down just take a deep breath and try to relax. Know that one day you will be the one looking at another new mommy with those same friendly eyes and a quiet, knowing smile.

Travelling with baby

Travelling with a young baby can be a difficult task, but there are a few tricks of the trade that seasoned mommies use when travelling with a baby.

By car - If possible leave as close to your baby's bedtime as possible. A long highway drive will lull your baby to sleep and hopefully keep him there until arriving at your destination. If your drive is too long to leave this late or you are not comfortable driving at night, instead leave close to your baby's naptime. In this case try not to let your baby sleep more than four hours, in effort to preserve his nighttime sleep. Take short breaks to feed and play with your baby every few hours. Giving your baby a chance to stretch out and play will help keep him comfortable and more content during the trip.

By plane - Airplanes can be hard on baby's ears, especially during takeoff and landing. Give baby something to suck on, like a pacifier, bottle, breast, or cup to help relieve the pressure. Also, bring a few small toys to keep him occupied during the flight. Avoid anything obnoxiously loud to keep him from disturbing the other passengers around you. Most importantly, especially if you and baby are travelling alone, make an airplane friend. It can be the person sitting beside you, the flight attendant, or a friendly-looking grandma seated near you. It usually isn't too hard to find at least one person who is captivated by your adorable little one. Look for someone who appears to be a parent themselves, but isn't traveling with any small children. By throwing out a few friendly looks, pleasantries, (and a smile or two from your baby never hurt) you'll land yourself a helper-to-be in no time. This person will be invaluable as your second set of hands to hold extra blankets, bottles, or help retrieve the toys your little monster tosses into the aisle. They can also be a nice sounding board to chat with or even share some advice.

I'd like to think my daughter gets her impeccable flirting technic from her mama. She is the best at zeroing in on her target, batting those incredible baby blues and cooing until an onlooker starts smiling back at her. I really appreciate how she can reel in a friendly helper when I'm travelling alone with her on an airplane.

Pack as little as humanly possible - We've all seen her. The martyr mom shlumping down the airport hallway or carrying bag upon bag to the car. She looks burdened, beyond tired, and a wee bit like nomatic hoarder. Up your style quotient and save your back by downsizing the luggage. Yes, babies come with a lot of things. However, you really don't need everything all the time. Think about yourself. You probably own a lot of beauty care products, but you don't take them ALL with you on a trip. The same goes for baby. To help slim down your travel case, think about two rules.

1. *Can I buy/borrow it there?* Things like diapers, wipes, baby food, maybe even a few inexpensive blankets, toys, or burp cloths can easily be purchased at your destination. If you don't need them for the trip and they are disposable or very inexpensive, consider just purchasing them when you arrive. You can donate anything unused to friends or a shelter before you leave. If you are visiting close family or friends, can you ask them to purchase or borrow a pack & play or umbrella stroller instead of bringing your own?

2. *Do I REALLY need it?* It is tempting to think you need all your baby gear. Try being a bit more creative. Our parents and grandparents survived raising children with a lot less. Surely you can survive for a few days without ALL your baby 'essentials.' If

you don't plan on going for many long walks, consider leaving the stroller at home and bringing your sling or baby carrier instead. Most infant car seats CAN work without the base. Learn to use yours this way and leave the base at home. If your baby is calm enough to eat on your lap, ditch the highchair for a few days and see what happens. Bring just a select few toys and books. Your baby will probably be just as happy playing with an empty bottle of water and the in-flight magazine. The less you have to carry, the happier you'll be.

Above all, don't be afraid to leave the house or travel with your baby. Life is short, and the time during which your child is a baby is even shorter. Even the longest trip is only a few hours of your life. Embrace the fierce, adventurous mommy spirit within you and start making memories that will last a lifetime.

CHAPTER 7

Relationships

HAVING A BABY changes your life. Most of us are prepared for getting up earlier and adding changing diapers to our daily routine. How a baby can drastically change our interpersonal relationships however, is often less expected. When lazy weekends with your spouse are suddenly replaced by watching your little one munch his books and lick his toys, you both might start to wonder what happened to the connection you shared back when it was just the two of you. As the leisurely lunches and shopping dates that you once took for granted start to evaporate, the energy it costs you to maintain relationships with your girlfriends may start to feel like more effort than they are worth. You'll sometimes question what you ever used to talk to your extended family about, now that the only thing on their mind is the baby. Around them you might feel like the invisible mother. That is, except for when they are offering unsolicited advice about how to raise your baby. After a few months of these changes, you might find that you no longer feel so fabulous.

Feeding your relationships is now as, if not more, important than ever before. While being a new parent can feel overwhelming and leave you with little time to nourish your relationships, you must make the effort. Having a strong support system to share your struggles and triumphs with will help you to build yourself into the extraordinary, confident new mommy you want to be.

Your partner

<u>*Carve out 1:1 time*</u> - As hard as it can feel to pull yourself away from the new love of your life, try to remember that before your little one arrived there was someone else you called baby. He still needs your attention as much as before, arguably more. Make it a priority to spend quality time together at least twice a month. Hire a babysitter, sweet talk a family member, or bribe a co-worker. Do whatever it takes to make sure you get time alone with your sweetie on a regular basis. At first it might feel strange, even awkward, to be alone without your baby. Just keep practicing. Like riding a bike your feelings for your spouse will come flooding back as you continue to create opportunities to spend quality time together. When you are spending time à deux, try to minimize talk about your sweetie-pie. If you must discuss her latest adorable development, try to get it out of your system during the first 15 minutes of your date then move onto other things.

1:1 time does not have to be a night on a proper date. Before we had a baby, my husband and I loved to ride bikes and play tennis on the weekends. For whatever reason we thought it was weird to get a babysitter so that we could go on a bike ride, so we kept alone time to mostly evening dinner dates. When my mom came to visit we were able to spend our first afternoon together and realized how much we missed that time. Now we hire sitters so that we can indulge from time to time in a daytime tennis match or trail ride. I think we are happier and more connected because of this. Find the things you and your spouse love to do together and try to incorporate these things into your dates.

Focus on the 80, not the 20 - While date nights are a great time to reconnect, the reality is that now the majority of the time you spend together is not going to be just the two of you. If you rely only on one-on-one time to keep the spark in your relationship it will be hard to keep the fire roaring for long. Instead, try to carve out time each day to focus on being together as a couple. It could be as little as five minutes. As long for those moments you are 100% focused on just one another.

If you can, try to put your baby to bed before 8:30pm. If you get into this habit you will have at least an hour each evening free to focus on one another. Use this time to reconnect instead of doing chores or recounting exactly when your baby napped or what she ate that day. Instead play a board game, chat over a glass of wine, make a late dinner, or cuddle up and watch your favorite program.

On the weekends, try new activities as a family. Couples bond when they experience new things together. Babies are a great excuse to check out new places. Explore your local aquarium, zoo, or children's museum. You might be surprised how much fun those places can be for adults too! At the very least, you will have created a new memory, and probably two-dozen new photos, that you can share for years to come.

Remember that by prioritizing each other you are not only helping your relationship, you are also benefiting your baby. Children crave harmony within the family relationship. They instinctively feel more confident and secure when they see their parents displaying love and affection for one another. Make a point to create a loving, positive example for your baby every day.

He's your partner, not your assistant - One of the toughest things for new parents to figure out is how to work *together* to care for a new baby. Since moms are typically the primary care givers it can be hard for us to give up control of major tasks like feeding, dressing, changing, and bathing the baby. Even though we are overwhelmed and could use some help, we're still not sure if Dad will do things *right.* A.K.A. how we would do them. So instead of giving him a major role in caring for the baby, we insist he assist us with ALL the tasks we are overwhelmed by. *Can you grab me a diaper so I can change the baby? Can you pour the bath so I can bathe the baby? Can you wash the bottles so I can feed the baby? Can you tidy up the kitchen so I can take a rest?* And so on. Unfortunately, this does not make Dad feel empowered as a parent and can become really frustrating for him. Avoid the temptation to make your husband your assistant. Instead collaboratively figure out how you can help each other.

Appreciate the efforts he is making to care for your baby and encourage his ways of doing things, even if those ways are not the same as yours. The more he feels that you acknowledge his efforts and trust him with the big stuff, the more he will want to contribute. As hard as it can be to relinquish control, it will be a thousand times better for you and your spouse if he becomes a true co-parent who takes full responsibility for the welfare of your baby. Doesn't that sound better than a helper who can pass you the wipes dispenser after a major diaper explosion?

Give him specific baby tasks - Try to avoid the temptation to have Mom do all the 'baby work', even if Dad works full time outside the house and it is Mom's job to stay home and raise the kids. There is a reason babies have two parents. Fathers need time to bond with their babies and to appreciate what it takes to care for them. Empower your husband to want to get more involved in your baby's life by ensuring that he has the opportunity to spend quality time with him.

Ideally each of you should have a few tasks that you are in charge of. Maybe Dad is the lead baby bather and Mom is the primary baby dresser. Perhaps Mom feeds the baby all day, but Dad gives the nighttime bottle. When it comes to diaper duty could you arrange that Mom changes the weekday diapers but on the weekend that is a Daddy duty? The more you both understand your roles, the less room you leave for disagreements and misunderstandings.

When you ask him for help, consider your approach. Appreciate that he may not feel as comfortable with many of the tasks as you do. Caring for a newborn isn't second nature to everyone. Many men need time and practice before they feel confident taking full ownership of a baby task. Be kind and caring in your approach and your relationship can only benefit.

Be direct - Men tend to respond better to specific ideas rather than general concepts. Therefore, it helps if you can be direct with your husband about what you want. For example, rather than asking him to help tidy up the house, ask him to empty the dishwasher and take out the garbage. Instead of requesting help with the bedtime routine, ask him to read the baby a story and give her a bottle. If you feel like romance is lacking in your relationship since the baby arrived, don't tell him he isn't making you happy anymore. Instead, tell him you would like him to plan a special night out for the two of you. Men like to understand what is expected of them, so try to clearly articulate what you want with as much specificity as possible. Wouldn't it be nice to be that simple?

Distinguish listening from problem-solving - As women, sometimes we just like to bitch. This is different than asking for help or looking for a solution. We are just talking because we want someone to listen or to sympathize with us. While this may be common code between you and your girlfriends, it can be very confusing to your man. As you are droning on and on, he is probably getting increasingly stressed trying to figure out how to calm you down. He will probably make suggestions that he thinks could help you, yet no matter what he proposes nothing seems to satisfy you. Of course this is because you aren't looking for a SOLUTION, you are looking for SYMPATHY! Or maybe just someone to listen. Before you know it, you are fighting and you aren't really even sure why. If you do have talks like these with your spouse, start them with either "I'm looking for your help with a problem..." OR "I'd like you to listen and comfort me..." This will clue your husband into if he needs to dive in and help you solve a problem or just provide a little understanding and TLC. You will both appreciate the increased clarity in your communication.

Use his problem-solving skills - Generally women love to talk about problems; men like to fix them and move on. Use your hubby's natural talent for solving problems by engaging him when you need help figuring something out. Brainstorming ideas together will help you discover more creative solutions and make both of you feel more involved in the decision-making process. It will also give him more ownership for the solution.

For example, if you are overwhelmed by housework ask him to help you come up with ideas on how to make cleaning the kitchen more manageable. If he proposes you hire a housecleaner or offers to clean the stove once a week, he will feel better about signing the check or scrubbing knowing it was his idea. When you are looking for sympathy, call your mom or your girlfriends. When you are looking for solutions, a heart-to-heart with your man can be just what the baby doctor ordered!

Your girlfriends

Embrace big events - Birthdays, graduations, house-warmings, weddings, and of course baby showers. When a girlfriend has a big event to celebrate, make a point of being there. After you have a baby, you probably won't see your girlfriends as much as you did before. Life tends to get busier and often you become less interested in the same activities as your childless friends. For this reason, make a big deal out of the few times you do still get together.

Schedule time to talk - Use your calendar to remind yourself to call your best girlfriends on a semi-regular basis. Try putting a note in your agenda every two weeks or so. Even if you don't have time to sit down and talk, leave a quick voicemail or send an email note letting her know you are thinking about her. If you have a baby blog or website, ask your girlfriends if they want to receive your posts. Even a little thing like this will help remind each of you of your friendship, and keep you abreast of what is going on in the other's life. Make a real effort to reach out to each of your good friends on a regular basis after having the baby. The longer you go without talking, the harder it will become to maintain the relationship over the long term.

Quality over quantity - Sadly, after becoming a mommy, your list of girlfriends may become a little more streamlined than before. After a few months you will realize which friends you really want to make an effort to stay in touch with. You will also see who is willing to make the same effort with you in return. Focus on maintaining these few quality relationships instead of killing yourself to keep all of them afloat.

Make new friends - If most of your girlfriends don't have children it's time to recruit some new mommy friends. Now that you have a baby, you may find it easier to relate to other moms because you are both in a similar life stage as new parents.

Mommy friends can be a wonderful source of support and advice, as well as the keepers of future playmates for your little one. To find new mommy friends, go where the mommies are! Check out local playgroups, baby classes, or even the park. Look for new friends that you have a genuine connection with. Relationships are likely to last longer when you have something in common beyond just your children's age.

Your extended family

Involve them - The birth of your baby is an incredibly exciting time for your family too. With all that is going on, it is easy to focus just on your immediate family and ignore the needs of everyone else. Instead try to involve your extended family, especially the grandparents, in any way you can. Ask your parents and in-laws what they want to be called (Grammy, Nana, Opa, Papa etc.), get their opinion on birth announcements, or ask for tips on how to get your little one to sleep. Even if you don't always take their well-meaning advice, they will appreciate being asked. Plus they'll probably never know you didn't implement all their suggestions anyways. Remember that your baby is special to many people in your family and they also want to feel like part of your sweetie's life.

Set boundaries - Especially around the birth of your baby, make sure to communicate your expectations to your family members. Do you want visitors immediately after birth? Would you prefer they visit in the hospital or at home? Are you hungry for advice or would you rather figure things out on your own? Do you hope people will pop over to see how you are doing, or do you prefer that they call first? Clarifying these things with family members will help ease tension that can naturally arise after the birth of a baby. The clearer you can be with your expectations, the more information you give your family. If you don't tell them what you want, they won't know! Speak up for the health of your relationship.

Schedule time - Unless you are the type that loves visitors showing up unexpectedly at your door, try to schedule time for family members to see your baby.

If the grandparents live close by, try offering to visit with them at a specific time, like after church every second Sunday. The appointment doesn't need to be written in stone and of course there may be other opportunities when you get together, but having a set time should help them feel secure that they will always have 'their time' with your baby. If you are comfortable leaving the baby alone with them, this can also double as a great opportunity for you and your spouse to have some time alone together.

For other family members, try to organize events when many of them can see the baby at once. Visiting with everyone can feel like a full-time job, especially if you have a large family. Getting everyone together at once is a more efficient way to spread the baby love around. Ask a family member if they are open to hosting a Sunday dinner or family BBQ. If no one has the quarters to accommodate try meeting at a local park for a picnic. Aim to participate in an event like this every two to three months.

If your family is not local, make a point to keep them involved with regular phone calls, email updates, and photos. And *Skype, Skype, Skype*! You can easily set up regular appointments to *Skype* with remote family members. They will love being able to see your little one grow up before their eyes. Make a point to connect with remote grandparents on at least a weekly basis. Time can fly as a new mommy; making notes to yourself will help remind you to reach out to make these important connections.

Yourself

You're a woman too! - After having a baby it can become easy to forget that you were a full, functioning person before you were a mama. You had dreams, ambitions, hobbies, and guilty pleasures just like everyone else. Guess what? You still do! Just because you are now a mommy does not mean you have to give up being who you were before the baby. It is imperative you find ways to nourish your needs alongside those of your little one. As hard as it is to believe that one day your little pumpkin will leave the nest, it will happen. You need to make sure that when it does, your life has been about more than just caring for your children. You can spend the next eighteen years defining yourself as only a mommy, or you can choose to have a full life within which being a mommy is one (large!) piece. The better habits you create now, the easier your transition will be when the big day comes. And the more fun you will probably have along the way.

Nap time = You time - Not laundry time, not bottle washing time, YOU time! Try to spend at least one of your baby's nap periods each day indulging yourself in something just for you. Take a long shower, work on your poetry, read a book, do a yoga DVD, give yourself a pedicure, do whatever your body feels it needs that day. Put yourself first once per day. Ideally try to do something that engages your mind or improves your body rather than veg'ing out in front of the TV. Yes, some days an episode of *Jersey Shore* is just what the doctor ordered, but try to keep this as the exception not the rule. If you spend all your free time watching TV and all your work time watching your baby, your life can become a bit one dimensional. Not to mention you'll become really boring to talk to. Suddenly the only things you have to add to a conversation are which

Real Housewife just got her boobs done and which foods turn your baby's poop orange.

Remember what you loved to do pre-baby and try to incorporate those things into your life a few times per week. For example, if you were always interested in technology, take an online web design course. If you loved pilates classes, try learning a new discipline like gyrokenesis with an at home DVD. If you liked cooking, experiment with new recipes. If you lived for spa days, try creating your own at home treatments with organic ingredients like avocado, olive oil, and glycerin. The sky is the limit as to how you spend your free time. The key is to use it!

Most people rolled their eyes at me when I told them I was writing a book while taking care of a new infant. They smirked that I would never have time to finish something so… discretionary. But writing fed my soul and gave me a sense of accomplishment, so I held myself to creating "me" time most days so that I could continue to progress towards my goal of finishing the book.

<u>Thou shall never do what can be done when the baby is awake, while the baby is sleeping</u> - A common trap that moms fall into is spending nap time doing chores and getting ready. If you do this, you will leave very little time for yourself. Neglecting yourself is the worst thing you can do for your relationship with you! Avoid it at all costs. If you have found a way to get a shower, vacuum, or do laundry when the baby is awake, then DO THESE THINGS WHEN THE BABY IS AWAKE! If you haven't figured how to do these things with baby in tow yet, then keep trying. This is probably the single biggest thing you can do to help maintain your sanity and create a little 'you time'.

My daughter loved sitting in her buzzy chair next to the shower and playing peek-a-boo with me while I washed my hair. So I made a point to never waste nap time showering. Likewise, many babies love slings or baby carriers. If your baby is agreeable, strap her on when you empty the dishwasher, throw in the laundry, or make lunch. She will love the snuggles and you will love that your chores are done before she goes down for her zzzzz's. When your baby gets older he will be able to sustain periods of independent playtime. Try putting him in his pack & play to amuse himself while you finish up whatever needs to be done. Don't ever waste a nap time!

Quiet moments - Try to take a few minutes each day to just be quiet. Sit and listen to your breathe enter and exit your body. Inhale deeply, close your eyes, and just be still. Even a few breathes can help calm and relax you. Some people find this easiest to do in the morning before the baby gets up. Others find they relish the break in the middle or at the end of the day. Take your quiet moments wherever you can, whenever you feel you need one. The adult-only zone in your home is a great place to escape for a quiet moment, as can be the shower or your bed just before you drift off to sleep.

Being a fabulous new mommy requires feeling like one. By nourishing the most important relationships in your life you are building a foundation that will support you during tough times and celebrate with you in great ones. The more time you invest in maintaining these relationships, especially the one with yourself, the better equipped you will be to flourish as your fabulous new mommy self.

Conclusion

WHEN I WAS pregnant everyone told me that becoming a mom would be a life-changing experience. Secretly, in my mind I hoped for the kind of life change that would unleash a new super-human, super-fabulous mommy goddess from inside of me. With these new powers I saw myself spending my maternity leave doing so many new and exciting things. I pictured myself running my first marathon, pushing my trendy jogging pram with a freshly manicured hand. I saw myself spending days at home turning out scrumptious chocolate chip cookies, clad in form fitting jeans and an adorable waist cinching apron, all with a baby on my hip. I was excited to find new stylish mommy friends to meet for midday walks and lattes. I could just see my precious new addition all snuggled up in her new charcoal-grey *Bjorn* cooing up at us at the local *Starbucks*. In the evenings, I imagined dazzling my husband with candles and dinner (OK honestly I pictured takeout) while our little one slept peacefully through the night. There it was, nestled in my mind: a picture perfect, super-stylish mommyhood.

Things didn't turn out exactly as I'd imagined. On the positive side, I did learn how to live as a new mommy without totally sacrificing my personal style. However, I also realized that despite my best efforts, some days I was just meant to clean diaper explosions from car seats with baby puke in my hair. I learned to take these setbacks in stride and found ways to insert fabulousness, or at least humor, into even the least fabulous situations.

The first time my daughter pooped in the bathtub, after getting over the shock and ick, I grabbed the camera and documented her smiling and splashing, poop and all. When she spat up on my sweater at the mall, I took it as a sign from the universe that is was time for a new even more gorgeous top.

The most important thing I learned was that by trying to maintain my stylish side, a somewhat shallow activity, I found myself actually starting to feel like a better mom. I noticed this about other woman too. In general, the mommies I met that prioritized themselves, at least somewhat, seemed to be happier and easier to be around than the ones that didn't. I don't think it's a stretch to believe that others close to them also felt the effect of their happiness, or lack thereof.

In Melody Beattie's book "Journey to the Heart" the author talks about how to restore your natural balance by managing your breathe. "Inhale, receive. Exhale, give back. Your natural balance is as necessary as breathing. The inhaling is the breathing in of life's energy. The exhaling is the sharing of your resources. You wouldn't expect to exhale if you hadn't inhaled ... You cannot give it out if you don't take it in." Simply brilliant. The same way we cannot expect to breathe out if we have not breathed in, we cannot expect to take care of those around us if we do not take care of ourselves first.

If we refuse to take moments just for us, to nurture the woman behind the baby, we are indeed doing a disservice to our families and whomever we come into contact with. Remember, you have to take care of YOU. By putting yourself first, you are actually helping yourself to better care for others around you. Put on your oxygen mask before assisting the other passengers.

For me, as superficial as it sounds, finding little ways to infuse style into my life makes me feel good. And I like to feel good! Some days it's a few extra moments fully blowing out my hair; others it's an hour experimenting with new ways to camouflage the baby toys within my décor scheme. Whatever it is that makes you feel good, do it! Finding time to connect with the woman you were before the baby is a great source of positive energy. For many women, reclaiming your personal style is a big piece of that puzzle.

At the end of the day, finding the exact right pair of distressed leather boots isn't what is important in life, and certainly not in parenting. (Unless of course you find a pair of *Cole Haan* boots with Nike Air Technology at a half off sample sale in your size. Those might qualify as important in your life, depending on how long you've been searching.) Fashion tips and beauty tricks are fun little escapes that can help you maintain your sense of self. Perhaps they'll even preserve a little bit of your sanity from time to time. Yet these aren't the things that will bring you the greatest joy in this chapter of your life.

Taking care of yourself creates a wonderful, virtuous circle. The more energy you have, the more you can put into caring for your baby. Showing love for your new little miracle is what will make you feel truly amazing. Nothing, certainly not a new tube of lip stain or a mani/pedi beats caring for your baby. To calm her when she is upset, comfort her when she is sick, tickle her until she giggles, or hold her when she is scared. When you show your baby how much you love him, you receive a reward unlike any other. It is worth keeping your energy tank full so you can keep fueling this amazing circle of love.

You now have the most important job on the planet. You're a mom. You've found a new center, a purpose. There is no amount of weight loss or spa time that can even come close to giving you the high you felt the first time your baby looked up into your eyes or cracked her first big gummy grin. It is now your awesome responsibility to love and look after this amazing little person, in the best way that only you know how. Take time to rejuvenate yourself so you have the energy to do the very best for your baby. But please, don't do it in high-waisted Levi's.

Acknowledgements and Gratitude

THIS BOOK WOULD not have been possible if it were not for many people and the support of my family and friends.

Most importantly, I want to express my eternal gratitude to my mother. For as long as I can remember, she has told me that I can do anything that I set my mind to. While everyone else told me horror stories about how becoming a mommy would turn me into a frustrated, time-starved crazy person who wouldn't be able to shower or sleep, she encouraged me. She told me I could become whatever kind of mommy I wanted to. That it was up to ME to determine who I was going to be.

I am deeply grateful to my husband for showing me what truly unconditional support looks like. Calvin, you indulged my (one too many) conversations about mommy beauty tips and fitness regimes, and read countless versions of my gushy girly writing; but more importantly you encouraged and supported me in ways that no one else could. It was you that gave me the confidence to make an idea a reality. Thank you for being my partner on this crazy journey. I've loved living every chapter with you.

Many people I've never met in person have inspired me deeply and played an important role in the creation of this book. Robert Collier, Oprah Winfrey, Melody Beattie, Rhonda Byrne, James Redfield, Paulo Coelho, and Wallace Wattles, thank you for your words of inspiration. You are changing (my) world!

Carey Corp and Krista Neher – thank for your publishing expertise and sharing your wisdom with me.

All the mommies, especially Jessica Wellinghoff and Angela Alvarez – thank you for reading my early drafts, I can't express how much your encouragement and feedback meant.

Dad – You taught me that nothing is impossible. Your steady words of encouragement made me feel like I could never fail. I appreciated your belief in me more than you could ever appreciate. Thank you for teaching me that if you never try, you'll never know.

Jay – without our "chats" I'm not sure where in my life I'd be. You are a wise beyond your years and a driving force behind my accomplishments. I love you.

My Pampers family – Thank you for your passion for parenthood and the insight and understanding you've brought to my life.

Words cannot come close to expressing the love and gratitude I've discovered after the birth of my amazing daughter, Mackenzie. Without you there truly would be no book. You are the inspiration behind every chapter, every sentence. You've changed my life. You are my purpose. I hope you are proud of your mommy.

CPSIA information can be obtained at www.ICGtesting.com
Printed in the USA
LVOW072011270412

279463LV00025B/38/P